JESUS IN MY SHOES

Other Books by Lori Peckham

Insight Presents More Unforgettable Stories
(compiled with Chris Blake)

Other Books by Tim Lale

Ten Who Left (with Fred Cornforth) (Pacific Press)
Ten Who Came Back (with Pat Habada) (Pacific Press)

To order listed titles and additional copies of *Jesus in My Shoes,* by Lori Peckham and Tim Lale, call **1-800-765-6955.**

Visit us at www.rhpa.org for more information on Review and Herald products.

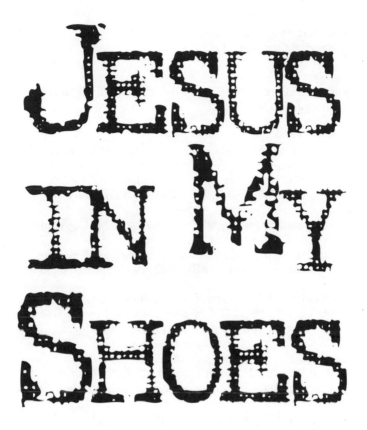

JESUS IN MY SHOES

Lori Peckham and Tim Lale

REVIEW AND HERALD® PUBLISHING ASSOCIATION
HAGERSTOWN, MD 21740

The authors assume full responsibility for the accuracy of all facts
and quotations as cited in this book.

Unless otherwise credited, Bible references are from the *Holy Bible,
New International Version*. Copyright © 1973, 1978, 1984, International
Bible Society. Used by permission of Zondervan Bible Publishers.

Texts marked Clear Word are from *The Clear Word*, copyright © 1994
by Jack J. Blanco.

Bible verses credited Message are from *The Message*. Copyright © 1993.
Used by permission of NavPress Publishing Group.

Scripture quotations marked NASB are from the *New American Standard
Bible,* © The Lockman Foundation 1960, 1962, 1963, 1968, 1971, 1972, 1973,
1975, 1977.

Scriptures marked NLT are taken from the *Holy Bible*, New Living
Translation, copyright © 1996. Used by permission of Tyndale House
Publishers, Inc., Wheaton, Illinois 60189. All rights reserved.

This book was
Edited by Richard W. Coffen
Copyedited by James Cavil
Designed by Bill Tymeson
Cover design by Trent Truman
Typeset: 12/14 Times

PRINTED IN U.S.A.

01 00 99 98   5 4 3 2 1

R&H Cataloging Service
Peckham, Lori Lee, 1962-
    Jesus in my shoes, by Lori Peckham
and Tim Lale.

    1. Teenagers—Prayerbooks and devotions—English.
I. Lale, Tim, 1964-   , joint author.   II. Insight.   III. Title.

242.683

ISBN 0-8280-1336-5

Dedication

To my parents, Don and Ann Lale, who lived and died
holding firmly to things hoped for and not seen.

Tim

To my parents, Lee and Ellen Tripp, who have helped me
and so many others follow what Jesus would do.

Lori

Contents

Born Lucky

I was born lucky. At least that's what my grandpa always told me. And he seemed to be right. I mean, just about every time I put my finger into a vending machine or telephone coin return slot, I'd feel something thin and cold. A dime. Or a nickel. Sometimes even a quarter.

I'd run to Grandpa and show him, and he would grin. After all, he'd taught me to check those places.

Then there were all the friends I made every time we went to the beach. Grandpa would build fancy castles with our picnic supplies: turrets from paper cups, flags from straws and napkins, bridges from Popsicle sticks. Kids would gather around, and I'd get a bunch of playmates for the afternoon.

And there was the summer I was 16. I'd just broken up with my first boyfriend and went to visit my grandparents. Usually I loved being at their home by the ocean, but this year I felt pretty depressed.

Grandpa and I were walking the beach one day when someone yelled, "Hi, Lori!"

I looked up and around. Two lifeguards were smiling and waving from their lifeguard stand. Then I saw one give Grandpa a high sign.

And suddenly things began to dawn. I laughed.

"Grandpa, how do they know my name?" I asked.

He shrugged.

"You wouldn't happen to have anything to do with it?"

Again he shrugged.

And then I began to put all the years of "luck" together. The coins in the return slots. The kids who came around. The lifeguards' greeting.

Grandpa had been behind it all. Sneaking his pocket change into the slots. Creating fun activities that would attract playmates for me. Telling the lifeguards that his granddaughter needed a friendly hello.

Grandpa planned special surprises for me—just like God does. Every day God places things in our path to make us feel happy and loved. Maybe a beautiful sunset. An open talk with a parent. A laugh with a friend. A passage in the Bible.

He works at making life better for us, and every good thing we encounter every day comes from Him.

Yeah, Grandpa was right. I *was* born "lucky." All of us were.

"Every good and perfect gift is from above, coming down from the Father of the heavenly lights, who does not change like shifting shadows" (James 1:17).

Lori

I Just Didn't Get It

Confession time. One of the things that bugged me growing up was that, perhaps from the example of people around me, I viewed the Bible as a rulebook. No matter how many sermons I heard about Jesus' love, I never experienced it, because I thought the rules came first and then the love came afterward.

I believed this until even after my teenage years. Even though I got baptized when I was 16, I still hadn't figured out that God wanted to *give* me His love and *give* me His Son's sacrifice.

My parents and teachers probably tried to convince me about God's unconditional love, but I sensed that they wanted to get past that to the obedience part, which seemed to interest them more. In a sense, I wasted all those years I could have spent enjoying the peace of God's active love.

Nobody has to tell me to obey God now. I want to because I know God as a person. He deserves to be obeyed because everything He asks has a perfectly good motive behind it.

God is infinitely smarter than any of us, and also He's infinitely more giving and loving than any of us. I don't know how I missed this for so long. I used to think I had a working brain. But it woke up only a couple of years ago.

You might ask me, "Do you doubt God's goodness because He let you wait so long and battle so hard before you found out what He has to offer?" No, I can't doubt God's motive just because I won't know *how* He works behind the scenes until I get to heaven.

I'm certain God knew the right time to ask me if I was interested in His way. Has He been talking to you lately?

"The wind blows wherever it pleases. You hear its sound, but you cannot tell where it comes from or where it is going. So it is with everyone born of the Spirit" (John 3:8).

Tim

No Parking

The first time I took my driving test, I failed because I obeyed the signs. (Really.)

Learning permit in hand, I practiced in my parents' old Ford. Unfortunately, the morning of my driving test my dad had the car worked on. He wanted to make sure it was in good condition.

The mechanic adjusted the acceleration, which I found out as soon as the driver's license examiner got in the car and told me to take off. I touched the gas pedal, and we jerked forward.

In my shock I slammed on the brake. The car came to a dead stop, but the evaluator and I kept going. Oops.

After some more jerky stops and goes, the evaluator told me to return to the Department of Motor Vehicles parking lot. I was pretty sure I was a borderline fail.

"Just park over there," she said gruffly, looking down at her clipboard.

I stared at where she was pointing. A sign clearly said: "NO PARKING."

"Um, I don't think I'm supposed to park there," I squeaked.

She didn't look up but continued writing. "Just park there," she barked.

"But—" I began. One of my friends had told me that the evaluator might try to trick me. *Yes, this must be a trick to decide whether I pass or fail.*

"Ma'am," I almost whispered, "the sign says not to park there."

This time she looked up, slammed her fist on the clipboard, and then wrote big letters across my score sheet: FAIL. "I've never seen anything like this," she yelled, getting out of the car.

I met my mom in the waiting area. She could tell by the look on my face that I wasn't getting a license that day.

As we drove away, I showed her the sign: NO PARKING. But suddenly I noticed the small print below that: "Official DMV vehicles only."

I guess the evaluator wasn't trying to trick me after all. And I'm glad God never does. He gives us clear rules, and they're the keys to our success.

"When tempted, no one should say, 'God is tempting me.' For God cannot be tempted by evil, nor does he tempt anyone; but each one is tempted when, by his own evil desire, he is dragged away and enticed. Then, after desire has conceived, it gives birth to sin; and sin, when it is full-grown, gives birth to death. Don't be deceived, my dear brothers" (James 1:13-16).

Lori

Preach It!

I was 14 years old the first time I stood in front of a whole church. It was the academy church, and my classmates sat in the pews in front of me.

I had a simple assignment—stand up at the end of Sabbath school and announce where the classes would meet. I felt excited and important until the moment I faced the crowd. Then the room caved in on me, and my legs began rapping on the podium.

Two of the classes were taught by schoolteachers. Wouldn't you know that their names were Watson and Hankins. So I tried to tell everyone where Mr. "Watkins" would meet with his class.

I walked out of church shaking as though someone had tried to toss me off a 300-foot bridge. And I knew I had failed in my assignment when kids started asking me where they were supposed to meet. They hadn't understood a word of my announcement.

Now that I look back, though, I realize that from the way they were asking me, none of them had noticed I was so nervous. They didn't care. They just wanted information. I was the one with a nerve problem.

Since that day I've stood up in church and other places hundreds of times. I'm not a trained speaker, but with practice I've at least learned how to keep my words straight. I get a little nervous before speaking in public, but that never seems to go away altogether, even for famous preachers.

In your life with God you will almost certainly have opportunities to stand up front and share with a group. If you've been on one of *Insight*'s mission trips, you've already had that experience. If the thought of it makes you afraid, or you feel you can't do it when someone asks, send a prayer up to God for the strength. He wants you to take these opportunities and use them to glorify Him.

I've read that lots of people fear public speaking more than they fear anything else. I found out that you don't have to stay under this cloud. It doesn't need to be a self-fulfilling prophecy for you.

And if your knees betray you, I guarantee almost no one will notice.

"When you come together, everyone has a hymn, or a word of instruction, a revelation, a tongue or an interpretation. All of these must be done for the strengthening of the church" (1 Corinthians 14:26).

Tim

5
Let's Be Neighbors

When I was a kid my best friend lived right across the street. Her name was Lisa.

But there was one thing wrong with Lisa. We'd be happily bobbing in her swimming pool or romping on her swing set when her mom would open the screen door and shout out the dreaded words: "Time for Mister Rogers!"

Lisa would dash off to watch her favorite television show, while I'd be left playing alone for a whole half hour.

Now, don't be too hard on Lisa. She did invite me to watch with her—a bunch of times. But I refused. I just knew I couldn't like a man who took my playmate away from me every afternoon. So I vowed *never* to watch Mister Rogers *ever*.

Well, I broke my vow a few years ago and watched an episode. It wasn't so bad. One thing the man in the cardigan said really stuck with me. He asked us, his audience, "Won't you be my neighbor?" It was really like he was saying, "Won't you be my friend?"

When I heard that, I felt bad for getting mad at Lisa every afternoon. Who knows, maybe her time with Mister Rogers helped her be a better neighbor and friend to me. 'Cause she was really nice—loyal and sweet and unselfish with her toys.

I wonder, too, if spending time with Jesus doesn't make me a better neighbor and friend. He tells me important things like "Love your neighbor as yourself" and even "Love your enemies." He challenges me to go back out to the swing set or pool and be like Him.

So I forgive Lisa for watching Mister Rogers every day. Maybe she even taught me something about daily devotional time—putting it before everything else. Yeah, I'm glad we were neighbors.

"Very early in the morning, while it was still dark, Jesus got up, left the house and went off to a solitary place, where he prayed" (Mark 1:35).

Lori

I Know What I Want

My parental units owned a boring station wagon. They wore kinda boring, inexpensive clothes. My dad always wore a tie.

I did not want to be like this. No way.

My mom and dad worked for the church. They just did their jobs and didn't want to be well known or rich or noticed by church members or leaders or have lots of power to change things or influence people.

I did not want to be like this. No way.

Starting when I was about 12, I wanted to dress real sharp and work in a bank and drive a huge Mercedes. This is the picture I had of myself in the future. Be like my fuddy-duddy parents? No way.

It was fun to dream. If you had tried to tell me right then that God knew about something even *better* than my dream, I wouldn't have listened to you. I wanted the cars, the job, the clothes, the respect. Especially the cars.

What are the most important things in your life? What drives you? What do you really, really want in your future? You don't get answers to these questions overnight, because you gradually learn what's best for you over a period of years.

Later in my teen years I began to realize that I liked the love and attention my parents gave me. Noticing the pain and loneliness of some of the other kids at school, I wondered if I would want my dad to trade the station wagon for a Mercedes if it meant harming our family. Would I want my mom to buy expensive clothes if that might become more important to her than what my brother and I needed?

After a few more years I began to see what God thought was important for my life. He didn't push me to work my tail off for a Mercedes; He pointed me toward feeling happy and fulfilled, because He, the owner of everything, loves me and wants to give me what I need.

Wherever you're at right now with your dreams for the future, I can recommend from experience that God will have the best package of all.

"The god of this age has blinded the minds of unbelievers, so that they cannot see the light of the gospel of the glory of Christ, who is the image of God" (2 Corinthians 4:4).

Tim

7
Too Little

"We're here!" my grandfather announced proudly.

I looked at the white, rustic church he had parked in front of and wondered why he sounded so enthusiastic. But I followed my grandparents into the dimly lighted hallway.

"So this is your granddaughter!" a woman squealed, wrapping her arms around me. "Oh, isn't she precious?"

I hadn't been called that in years, so I just stood there and smiled sweetly.

Soon more people rushed us, exclaiming, "How nice to have you here for the summer! We couldn't wait to meet you!"

I was glad to escape into the sanctuary, which wasn't much larger than my bedroom at home. The song service was under way. It was led by a woman with a heavy German accent who sang flat. Yet her joy was contagious, and I found myself joining in (with the other 10 people there).

The next week the Sabbath school superintendent approached me. "Dear, we can't wait to hear your lovely voice. Would you lead the song service this morning?"

These people seem to assume that anyone who can walk can sing! I thought. But I said Yes, even though I wouldn't have considered it at my large home church.

The next week they asked me to play the piano, and by the end of the summer I had given Scripture and prayer, told the mission story, even taught the lesson. I used every talent I had and some I didn't know I had and some I just didn't have.

Every week I asked God to help me do what I'd been asked to do. "I know I'm asking a lot, God," I'd pray, "so at least deafen their ears or cause their hearing aids to fail."

One Sabbath near the end of the summer a few things dawned on me. I realized that this tiny, "lifeless" church had been a place for me to grow and come alive. And I understood that God recognizes the praises and prayers of a few worshipers in a little old church as much as He does those of many in a large, modern one.

The last Sabbath of the summer I took my regular spot on the piano bench. As I played the opening hymn, I watched the radiant faces of the congregation. I hit some wrong notes on the piano, and I heard some off-key voices, but in its own unique way the music was beautiful.

And I knew God was listening.

"Everyone who has [talents] will be given more, and he will have an abundance. Whoever does not have, even what he has will be taken from him" (Matthew 25:29).

Lori

He's Coming, All Right

During my teen years my mom and dad were teachers at an Adventist academy in Zimbabwe, in southern Africa. A war was going on around the edges of the country. It wasn't a huge war with bloody battles, but a terrorist war with small skirmishes between terrorists and the army. Many civilian people, Black and White, were killed throughout the eight years of this war.

In 1980 Zimbabwe became an independent country. The war faded away, and everyone looked forward to a peaceful future.

At the end of 1980 I flew back to England to go to academy there and finish my schooling. My brother had to move into the dorm at the Zimbabwe academy because my parents moved to an isolated mission school called Nyazura.

Two months after that, even though the war had been over for a year, two terrorists who had been indoctrinated to kill White people walked onto the Nyazura campus and forced one of the Black teachers to show them where the White people were. My parents were the victims, and died in the bloodshed.

I was 16 then. You can imagine how many questions I had. It took many years to answer some of them. I especially wondered why God was taking so long to come back. But He doesn't worry about time like we do.

The first Adventists experienced bitter grief one night in 1844 because Jesus didn't come to earth when they thought He would. It might have seemed like a mean trick to some people, but Jesus plainly tells us in the Gospels that no one knows the exact time of His return.

Some of those first Adventists kept their faith in spite of the trauma. I'm absolutely certain it will pay off.

Do you have someone you want to see in heaven? I'd like to introduce you to my parents there.

"I tell you the truth, you will weep and mourn while the world rejoices. You will grieve, but your grief will turn to joy" (John 16:20). "Now is your time of grief, but I will see you again and you will rejoice, and no one will take away your joy" (verse 22).

Tim

The Great Lost and Found

We talked about his thick eyebrows and how they arched when he kindly asked us if we'd like to move to California. I guess that's what a fourth and eighth grader notice about a conference president.

21

"And did you see how excited Mom looked?" my older sister, Teri, asked.

I'd lived with Teri for my 9 years of life. I knew she was feeling betrayed. "Yeah," I answered angrily. "I bet she wants to go."

"And Dad, too. I know we're going. That's the end of everything." Teri's voice cracked, and I knew she would cry if she didn't get the bitterness back.

We walked another lap around the school track. It was October. Snow would soon cover the New Jersey field in white. We loved the snow.

"What do you think it's like in California?" I ventured.

"I don't care!"

We were pastor's kids. We should have been used to the visits from conference presidents, the family discussions and prayers for guidance, Dad's sadness in preaching those last Sabbath sermons, the house full of boxes, the moving vans, the house hunting, those first days at a new school.

But this time we were more settled. We had our friends across the street, our friends at school, our own rooms. Besides, they wanted us to move before Christmas. That meant we'd have to go to a new school in the middle of the year. Moving at the beginning of school was bad enough.

"Maybe Mom and Dad don't know we don't want to go," I said. "Maybe when they find out—"

"They know. It was kind of obvious when we stormed away from the dinner table. Maybe I can stay here . . . " Teri began. "Maybe I can live with Cora Lee."

"Well, I'm staying too, then."

But two months later all four members of the family began the drive across the United States. Cora Lee wanted Teri to stay and live with her. But adults always stick together. Cora Lee's mother said Teri better go with her family.

So she did. So I did.

When we got to California we were surprised. The radio stations played the same songs we'd heard in New Jersey. They had McDonald's, Dairy Queen, and public libraries. Even though there was no snow, the people put up Christmas lights and evergreens, the church went Ingathering, and the school held a Christmas program.

We missed our friends. We missed our rooms, the town, and sledding. But happily, we found that many of the things we liked best about life were still around, like books and stuffed animals and music. There were new classmates with whom we began to share the elements of friendship we'd lost: companionship, laughter, secrets, pastimes. The sun still shone, and we found that we could travel.

Sometimes I think back on that move and think of moving to heaven. Leaving this earth is going to be pretty dramatic. And it's hard to imagine that we won't feel the slightest loss, because we like much of what we have. We cherish the things and the people we know.

So we ask questions—with a hint of sentiment in our voices—such as: Will my boyfriend be there? How about skiing? Will I have close, special friends, or will everyone mean the same to me? Can God handle my kind of music? Can we still have TV, waterbeds, sports cars, and ice cream?

When I start asking questions like that, I remember how well God knows me. How He knows the things I love best here. And how in some ways entering heaven will be like entering a huge lost and found.

There we'll rediscover the good things we've felt and lost: incautious love, purity, trust, worth. We'll talk again with the people we loved and who died or with whom we lost touch.

The way we laughed on earth will seem like an echo of the laughter we will make there. Our running and singing and playing will be the real side of our clumsy, cautious earthly movements.

I believe that we will feel at home in heaven. We may not find McDonald's and Dairy Queen and the Top 40. But the best we've known will be there—better and forever.

Just before Jesus left earth He spoke to His disciples about when He would come again. He promised: "I will not leave you as orphans; I will come to you. . . . On that day you will realize that I am in my Father, and you are in me, and I am in you" (John 14:18-20).

Sometimes we forget that we're not the only ones who feel loss and homesickness. Our Father also waits for that day when we who have been lost (and have lost) will be found. He's eager for our coming back home to the great lost and found, where He has kept every good thing for us.

"Do not let your hearts be troubled. Trust in God; trust also in me. In my Father's house are many rooms; if it were not so, I would have told you. I am going there to prepare a place for you. And if I go and prepare a place for you, I will come back and take you to be with me that you also may be where I am" (John 14:1-3)

Is God for Real?

I didn't get baptized in a muddy pool, even though it happened in Gweru, Zimbabwe. The suburban church in which I went under the water was new and modern-looking, and it had carpet and padded pews.

I had just turned 16 when I got baptized. That seems kind of late to some people, but I hadn't wanted to do it in earlier years, and my parents respected my wish. At 16 I thought I was ready.

I should have been suspicious of my decision for a couple of reasons. First, I studied in a Bible group at academy with my girlfriend. I thought I had made my own decision to join the church, but I realized later that I had followed my girlfriend's lead. You have to discover your own pearl, if you know what I mean.

The other big problem was that I didn't know God. He hadn't become real to me. Sure, I knew a lot *about* Him. The pastor even gave me a certificate for learning a bunch of Bible stuff. But somehow I missed the point that God is alive, that He was in the room, watching.

So I gradually drifted away again. A year later I gave up, thinking

I couldn't force myself to continue. And I was right. You get nowhere as a Christian without knowing God.

Joining the church is important, but it's only one small step in becoming a Christian. You take the first giant step when you understand that God is a real, living being whom you can get to know.

If you haven't taken that step yet, I can tell you that you'll discover a Being who's much cooler than you ever imagined. And the whole Christian thing will start to make sense.

"Jesus replied, 'If anyone loves me, he will obey my teaching. My Father will love him, and we will come to him and make our home with him'" (John 14:23).

Tim

Proof of Love

When I was 16 I had my first boyfriend. His name was William. We loved being together—and hated to part.

When William would take me home after a date, we'd stand on the porch, holding hands, not wanting to pull away. Sometimes he would get halfway down the walk and come running back. Sometimes I would chase his MG convertible down the street. My parents would sit in the kitchen and mutter, "They're going to see each other tomorrow morning at school."

One spring Sunday William and I returned from the beach. My father was mowing the lawn, so we cut our goodbye short. We felt cheated. So as William pulled away, I stood on the front lawn, waving and blowing him kisses.

He turned and waved back and caught my kisses, and then—*crash.*

I stared. Then I screamed. My father stopped the lawn mower. I ran to William.

He walked around to the front of his MG. Then he put his face in his hands and groaned.

He had hit the Oldsmobile parked in front of our neighbor's house. Pointing to the car's crumpled trunk and his MG's shattered headlight, he wailed, "My dad's going to kill me."

I felt sorry for William. And I knew we wouldn't be able to drive to the beach for a while.

Yet I couldn't shake this feeling of flattery. A guy had ruined a car for me. For one last glimpse of my face, someone had done $2,600 worth of damage to his prized MG. It was very romantic.

During the time we dated, William gave me some nice gifts—a book, a gold pin, a flower lei from Hawaii. But the gift of his wrecked car stands out.

And as I've read the Gospels, I've begun to feel the flattery of God's gift to us on the cross. Yes, God gives us gifts every day—like sunshine and laughter. But His greatest proof of love was allowing His most precious possession—His Son—to be scarred and broken for us.

That's the best romance you'll ever know.

"For God so loved the world that he gave his one and only Son, that whoever believes in him shall not perish but have eternal life" *(John 3:16).*

Lori

The Shooting

A six-foot chain-link fence and three strands of barbed wire surrounded the academy I attended in Zimbabwe. An alarm system ran through it, linked to a siren on the roof of the music teacher's house, next door to our house. With a war going on around us, we wanted at least a little warning if our school were to be invaded.

On windy nights the alarm sounded every time a strong gust came through; sometimes there would be a half-dozen false alarms in one night. Each time it blared, the music teacher's husband, Pat, had to get up and walk around campus until he found the security guard, who was supposed to know what was going on. Pat belonged to the army reserves, so he'd take his FN semiautomatic rifle.

Just after midnight one night, the siren started whining. Pat crawled out of bed, picked up his FN, and walked from his house toward the flagpole in the center of campus to look around. He could make out a figure standing outside the main gate, so he yelled as loud as he could for the person to identify himself. Silence. Pat yelled the same command in the African language of that area. Still no answer.

So Pat raised his rifle and fired. The figure let out a yelp and fell down. Pat went back to bed. I slept through the whole thing.

I heard about the shooting in class the next morning, and I heard the conclusion of the matter too. At dawn Pat had gone up to the gate and found a half-dressed, unarmed Zimbabwean soldier asleep in the grass outside the gate. He had a cut on his left arm where Pat's bullet had grazed him. When the guy woke up, he couldn't tell Pat where he was from. Apparently he was a little mentally unbalanced and had wandered away from his base. Pat gave him a ride into town.

I learned some things about protection while I lived inside that fence. The siren and the gun were there to help protect us from physical harm. But they could not win the war or change the hearts of people. Only God's hand provides absolute protection from the attacks of the devil. We've learned how to shield ourselves from some of the pains and accidents of life, but only God can protect us from eternal death.

"Do not be afraid of those who kill the body but cannot kill the soul. Rather, be afraid of the One who can destroy both soul and body in hell" (Matthew 10:28).

13

The Big C

"Your friends are upstairs talking about friendship," he began. "You're here to learn about the Big C."

The youth of our church had gotten out of bed before their parents this Saturday morning. Wearing jeans and toting lunch bags, we'd met at the church parking lot.

We'd driven the hour and a half into the city, meeting up with vanloads of teenagers, some displaying handmade "Grow for It" signs in their windows. We were going to the all-day "Grow for It" seminar put on by Youth Specialties.

That morning we sat in a large church in an old neighborhood of Baltimore. We sat with hundreds of teenagers from nearly every denomination. We sang together, laughed, played games, and listened.

Then we had to choose between two talks: "How to Be a Radical Friend" and "Totally Committed" (for people who were really serious about getting a closer relationship with God).

The group for "Totally Committed" packed the downstairs fellowship room. And then we started talking about the Big C.

"How do we know someone's committed to a sports team?" the speaker asked. "Anyone?"

"You go to practice," came an answer.

"How can we tell if someone's committed to a dating relationship?"

"They treat the other person with respect."

"Faithfulness."

"They make time to be together."

"You're describing behavior, right?" the speaker clarified. "Now how do we know if someone's committed to Christ?"

"His attitude."

"She prays."

"His love for others."

"Where her priorities are."

Kids were talking all around us.

"Good. Now let me take you on a roller coaster ride," the speaker continued. "You're at an amusement park. You stand in front of the roller coaster. You've read the signs (you're not pregnant, and you don't have heart trouble—you pass). You've checked the height chart (you're tall enough). Still, you hear blood-curdling screams coming from up above. What do you do?"

"You go on it," a guy piped in.

"OK, you make a decision to get on that roller coaster. You walk to the cars, sit on the seat, and pull the protective bar over you. The moment of committing yourself ends right then."

The room was silent a moment. "You see," he continued, "commitment is putting ourselves in a position where we won't back out. It's even making steps so we can't back out. Do you understand?"

The room was even quieter.

"We think life should be fun and easy. If it works and it's what we want, fine—we'll be committed to it. But as soon as it gets hard and painful, people tend to back out. That's not commitment."

"You're dead then," someone mumbled.

The speaker nodded. "Yes, you can't back out of a roller coaster ride very easily—especially once you're moving. But people back out of a lot of other things—for all kinds of reasons. *Commitment is sticking with something when it no longer seems worth it.* Got that? Even when it looks like there's no hope. That's commitment."

Wow. This was new. We—the audience—were kids from divorced homes, kids who had dropped out of school, kids who had stopped going to church, kids who had written off friends.

"Let's look at Jesus' commitment," the speaker continued. "When He decided to become human for us, He became committed. Without backing out. He stayed committed through calluses, indigestion, and stubbed toes. Committed through unpopularity, frustration, and death."

We had serious faces at that moment. The speaker looked at us. "Remember when Jesus was in Gethsemane the night before He was crucified? He suffered horrible pain and fear. In that moment He wanted to back out. He prayed, 'If it's possible, let this cup be taken from Me; *nevertheless,* not My will, but Your will.' That was commitment."

Suddenly we realized what Jesus had done for us, what the Big C really is about.

"Commitment," the speaker concluded, "is hanging out there further than ever before, with no turning back. Can you make that kind of commitment to Jesus now? Commitment to make Him a priority in your life, commitment to stick with Him when it's not fun and easy, commitment to grow in your relationship?"

We wanted to say yes. Not because we knew we would always be happy for that commitment, but because it was right. And what's right ultimately makes us happy.

The Big C is a big thing indeed.

"He was oppressed and afflicted, yet he did not open his mouth; he was led like a lamb to the slaughter, and as a sheep before her shearers is silent, so he did not open his mouth. By oppression and judgment he was taken away. And who can speak of his descendants? For he was cut off from the land of the living; for the transgression of my people he was stricken. He was assigned a grave with the wicked, and with the rich in his death, though he had done no violence, nor was any deceit in his mouth" (Isaiah 53:7-9).

Lori

Frankly, My Dear

Holding two full laundry baskets, I open the basement door and start walking down the stairs. I hit my head on the low ceiling and slip down the last five stairs. Clothes fly everywhere.

"*#% *@$* #!@&!!!!!"

I confess. Occasionally I cuss. Go ahead and judge me. Stone me. Throw me in the deep abyss. But have you ever slipped yourself?

The major excuse I hear from people is that those words come out when you're angry or hurt. Like if you're humiliated or injured or insulted, then it's OK. What's the big deal with cussing, anyway?

We probably all agree that using God's or Jesus' name as a cuss-word is out. No excuses ever for that. It really bugs me to hear it on TV. Network programs seem to enjoy rubbing it in our faces that they don't give a honk about God or Jesus. It's a shame that some people think it's cool.

But those other words, the biological ones that really satisfy sometimes. The problem with them is partly what the words mean, but it's more the attitude that motivates us to use them.

I use those words when I've lost my cool. I'm either frustrated or impatient or extremely annoyed. None of these sound like attitudes Jesus recommended.

Jesus talked about this problem of motives: "You're familiar with the command to the ancients, 'Do not murder.' I'm telling you that anyone who is so much as angry with a brother or sister is guilty of murder. . . . The simple moral fact is that words kill" (Matthew 5:21, 22, Message).

Strangely, whether I let those words fly in stressful situations depends on how I start the day. These days I usually remember to put myself in God's hands in the morning. So when I bruise myself up or get angry with somebody, God's Spirit in me will keep me from letting rip.

By the way, if you habitually cuss in ordinary conversation, remember the people around you. They wouldn't want to see you throw up. Why cuss all over them?

"So whether you eat or drink or whatever you do, do it all for the glory of God" (1 Corinthians 10:31).

Scaredy-cat

My cousin Lisa won't ride escalators. She's scared she'll fall down, and then the metal stairs will grab her as they close.

When Lisa and I go shopping in big department stores, we have to look for the elevator. And Lisa lives in New York, where every department store is big.

Every once in a while I forget about her fear and get on an escalator. When I look back she's still standing where I left her.

Uncle Calvin is scared of germs. Every time he eats in a restaurant he wipes his flatware with his napkin. Sometimes he dunks the flatware in his glass of water to rinse it. Sometimes he asks the waiter for a clean set. And he'll never eat from salad bars, because he doesn't trust the sneeze guards.

Everyone I know has fears of some kind, whether of nuclear war or mice. And I don't always react well to my friends' fears. Of course, they don't always react well to mine, either.

I'm scared of murder. Really, I'm scared of murderers. And the problem is that I can't tell a murderer from any other person I meet. So I'm scared of a lot of people I meet. I'm even scared of people I don't meet.

After the night stalker murders in Los Angeles, I was scared to stay home alone at night. When my roommate went on vacation, she wanted to set up an appointment for me to talk to a counselor about this fear. She said I had to face it.

Another friend told me that fear indicates a lack of faith in God. We need to trust that God will take care of us. We insult Him when we're scared.

Recently when I was scared that my next-door neighbor was a murderer, my friend Chris told me something important. God doesn't want us to be scared. And not because it insults Him. Because it hurts Him when we feel anxious.

He is our Father; we are His children. And He wants to comfort us as a father wants to comfort a child.

He is not angry or impatient with our fears, no matter how small-time and human they might be. He's sensitive to them. In the Bible when we read about God communicating to people Himself or through angels, we find Him consistently concerned about how they might react to such a visit.

Gabriel came to Mary with the news that she would bear a Son. The angel began with these words: *"Do not be afraid, Mary"* (Luke 1:30).

Angels appeared to the shepherds to declare Christ's birth. The shepherds were terrified, so an angel assured them: *"Do not be afraid. I bring you good news of great joy"* (Luke 2:10).

When Jesus walked on the water toward His disciples' boat, they cried in fear, "It's a ghost!" He immediately comforted them: *"Take courage! It is I. Don't be afraid"* (Matthew 14:27).

The women came to anoint Jesus' body after His death. They found the tomb empty and the stone rolled away. They were frightened. An angel appeared to them to say: *"Do not be afraid, for I know that you are looking for Jesus"* (Matthew 28:5).

The women hurried away to tell the disciples, and they met Jesus on the road. His first words to them were: *"Greetings. . . . Do not be afraid"* (verses 9, 10).

That evening when Jesus appeared to His disciples, they were shocked, and He said: *"Peace be with you!"* Again Jesus said, *"Peace be with you!"* (John 20:19, 21).

33

These texts tell me that our heavenly Father cares about our peace of mind. Whether our fears seem rational or not, grounded on evidence or all in our heads, God knows they are real to us. And that means they are important enough for His sympathy. Before trying to communicate to His children (and without making the least bit of fun), God quiets their fears.

I might think my friends' fears are dumb, and they might think mine are too. All the while Jesus says, "Come rest in My arms. And do not be afraid."

"I sought the Lord, and he answered me; he delivered me from all my fears" (Psalm 34:4).

Lori

School Daze

For part of my high school I was a day student, and for part of it I lived in the dorm at academy.

I liked the freedom and food at home, but the dorm residents seemed to be in on stuff I was missing. In the dorm I had not one, not two, but three roommates. How we got any sleep in between all the malarkey and snoring, I don't know.

Along the way in high school, I learned to play alto sax in the band, caught photography as an interest, got in a couple of fights (which I'd never done before), and learned the art of hitchhiking (don't try this). I ate outrageously bad food like peanut butter gravy on toast and huge gluten steaks. The choir and band trips were cool, and five or six of us played Beatles songs on the side, in a sort of ensemble.

At times academy life got electric. Like the afternoon I was standing under the shower after a soccer game. I'd gotten covered with mud and was the only one in the shower room. I didn't realize a thunderstorm had moved in after the game.

As I reached down and put my hand on the metal handle to turn the water up higher, I saw a bright flash. In the same second, a jolt threw my hand away. And the lights went out. Lightning had struck the building and spread through all the metal pipes.

Another enlightening experience was a Communion service in the cafeteria one Friday night. By the light of candles we ate some simple food and then sang choruses a cappella. In that darkened room with friends sitting around long tables, we got close to the experience of Jesus and His friends as He humbly offered His service to them. We were beginning to understand how Communion puts us in touch with Jesus.

My school wasn't perfect, and yours probably isn't either. But it's not there to be perfect. It's a great place to learn how perfect God's love is for you.

"Don't let anyone look down on you because you are young, but set an example for the believers in speech, in life, in love, in faith and in purity" (1 Timothy 4:12).

Tim

17

Summer School

The summer I was 16 I set three goals for myself.

1. I will run two miles on the beach every day.

2. I will lie in the sun till my brown hair bleaches blond and I get so tan I look like Malibu Barbie.

3. I will read my Bible every day.

My first boyfriend and I had just broken up that spring, and my parents sent me off to my grandparents to recover. (I was moping around and weeping a lot.) My grandparents lived near the beach in New Jersey, and they knew how to spoil me.

Well, can you believe it? I met all three goals that summer.

And I learned that goal-setting's a pretty good practice. Especially if you're motivated and choose a few attainable goals, it can really work. And it gives you a great sense of satisfaction when you discipline yourself to accomplish something you want to do.

I also learned, though, that some goals—in the long run—don't make a lot of difference in our lives.

The first goal I set, I believe, was good for me. I did feel really energetic and physically fit after jogging every day. And while I ran on the beach, some of my depression and sadness slipped off me and never came back. Exercise tends to do that, and I thank God for the ability to run and jump and walk.

But my motivation for exercising—just like my motivation for my second goal—wasn't the best: I wanted to look smashing when I got back so my ex-boyfriend would be sorry we weren't together anymore. That's why I wanted to be tan and blond and fit.

Well, our class did have a party at the end of the summer, and I got to wear my white summer dress and white sandals. He was there, and I felt pretty good about myself.

But now when I look at my photo album of that summer and read about skin cancer and hair damage, I think that was a pretty stupid thing to do. Things we do out of pride almost always are.

Goal number 3, though, has lasted. I have about five books of my Bible all marked up with detailed notes that I took that summer. I collected favorite Bible verses that still mean a lot to me. And I got to know God much better.

I'll never regret the summer I read my Bible every day. And that's how I want to remember it. Because what we do with God lives on. I have to remember that the next time I set goals.

"Heaven and earth will pass away, but my words will never pass away" (Matthew 24:35).

Lori

36

What's Your Phobia?

O ne Friday night my youth group had a gathering at the youth leader's house. Our leader kept a green parrot in a cage on top of a bookshelf. Someone took the parrot out, and it flew across the room. One of the girls, Trudy,* screamed and dived under a side table, where she stayed, trembling and complaining, until the parrot returned to its cage.

What was Trudy's problem? I think it might have been a form of zoophobia, which is the name for a fear of animals.

Some people have a chronic, paralyzing fear of the wildest things. If you are ailurophobic, you're deathly afraid of cats. Mysophobia is the overwhelming fear of dirt and germs. And nyctophobia, common among small children, is fear of the dark.

Ochlophobia is a good example of a phobia that can control a person's life. It's the fear of crowds. This fear might keep you away from football games, the mall, and maybe even church. If you are ophidiophobic and see a snake, your mind blanks out in total panic, and you run for your life.

And then there's my own personal phobia, xenophobia. The fear of strangers has bothered me, at least mildly, since I was very young. It makes meeting people difficult and is not a self-confidence booster.

These fears are deadly serious. They take away a person's reasoning power and cause them to panic as though their life were threatened.

Our faith in God may be severely challenged if we have to face a dreaded fear. Is it OK for us to run away from something we find so horrible? If not, what should we do?

If you have a serious phobia that controls your life, then you have an anxiety disorder that must be treated by a mental health professional. Don't feel that your faith is lacking if you suffer from such a disorder. There's evidence that some phobias are passed genetically, and all of them are caused by circumstances beyond the sufferer's control. As with drug addiction, phobias cannot be cured by the patient.

Even if you don't have a phobia, you may be afraid of something, and you probably don't want everyone to know about it. But God knows, and He doesn't leave you in the dark. He promises His love to anyone who believes in Him.

"There is no fear in love. But perfect love drives out fear" (1 John 4:18).

Tim

---
* Not her real name.

Thought I'd See You Again

I've seen fire and I've seen rain,
I've seen sunny days that I thought would never end,
I've seen lonely times when I could not find a friend,
But I always thought that I'd see you again.—James Taylor.

Tina wrote those words next to Tzu's picture in every yearbook she signed. You see, Tzu died his senior year in academy. And he was a good friend of Tina's.

I was a junior that year. And I remember when the horrible news came back from the senior trip.

The senior class had gone to the Grand Canyon. They'd hiked around rocky bluffs, swum in cold, clear pools of mountain water, and trekked up steep, dusty cliffs. Tzu and some friends went off exploring, and somehow Tzu fell off one of those high, sheer peaks. He was found at the bottom—dead.

It was right before graduation. So you can imagine that class night, consecration, graduation exercises, and Tzu's funeral all flowed together as companion events that spring. And commencement felt more like an end than a new beginning.

More kids showed up at Tzu's funeral than showed up at intramural basketball games. School closed for the morning. And I can still see his sister, a sophomore at the academy, rolling down the window of the hearse, tears streaming down her face.

We all dealt with death that spring. Most of us never had before. Especially the death of someone *our* age. And dying so quickly, so unexpectedly. Tina found what most of us felt in the lyrics of James Taylor's song. We just always thought that we'd see him again.

We always thought that we'd see *everyone* again. All our classmates. Our parents, our teachers, our friends. They'd just always be there.

We turned to God the spring of Tzu's death. As classes, as a school, and as individuals.

We realized how wonderful and unique each of our schoolmates was. Sure, the last measure of "Pomp and Circumstance" would perhaps send us off in different directions for a while, but death could interfere and separate us much longer. We needed to appreciate each other, love each other, help each other want to be in God's kingdom.

As a school we drew together. We had communal mourning. A special commemorative chapel program. A dedication page for Tzu rushed into the yearbook supplement. Mentions of him from the platform throughout graduation weekend. For Tzu was friendly, spiritual, and well-liked.

And we each mourned individually—in different ways, to different degrees, and for different reasons. Some of us cried because young people *can* die, because average life spans can't be counted on. Some cried for Tzu's sister; others for themselves.

Tzu's best friend, Mark, wrote a poem about the loss of an irreplaceable friend. He photocopied it for those who asked. And Tina never handed back someone's yearbook with only thoughts like "It was great knowing you this year! Take care, and have a nice summer."

Her words were much more important, meaningful, and encouraging. She wrote about how sad she was that our friendship with Tzu had been interrupted.

Because that's the overall conclusion we made of Tzu's death. That his life wasn't concluded. And that our friendship with him needn't be ended.

Sure, there would be lonely times. Horrible, wrenching, aching times for his family and close friends. And a twinge of someone missing at every school event. We all sort of expected he'd walk into school one day before the end of the school year, or show up at graduation. For no matter how thoroughly we comprehend that death means we won't ever see or touch a person again on this earth, we still often hope we will. And we're disappointed time and again.

But our mourning for Tzu was, for the most part, a spiritual one. A mourning of believers. Of teenagers who decided that although we hadn't been sure we even wanted to go to heaven (the right concept of heaven was something else we had to work out), maybe seeing Tzu again would be worth it. Maybe God just bringing all of us together again in a place where no one would ever die would be heaven enough.

Tzu's death turned us to hope. Because we were too young to believe that he was gone forever. And that tonight the same thing might happen to us and we'd be gone forever. No. That just isn't how God runs His universe.

We loved God then. And we depended on Him. We put Tzu into His trust. No one blamed God. I can't remember anyone being cynical or talking about the meaninglessness of life. We believed.

And I'm grateful for that. I know that everyone doesn't believe every time someone dies. And I know that in some circumstances it might be much harder.

But it helped us so much to believe. We looked to God, and He did come through. His promises comforted us. His heaven looked better to us. And we realized that God had done us the greatest act in saving us humans from eternal death and goodbyes.

"I always thought that I'd see you again," Tina wrote by Tzu's picture. I know for a fact that Tina still thinks she'll see Tzu again. So do most of us who knew him. And it will be a reunion high in the sky, a city on a mountain, with a flowing river of life. A place Tzu will like.

See you there, Tzu.

"Brothers, we do not want you to be ignorant about those who fall asleep, or to grieve like the rest of men, who have no hope. We believe that Jesus died and rose again and so we believe that God will bring with Jesus those who have fallen asleep in him. According to the Lord's own word, we tell you that we who are still alive, who are left till the coming of the Lord, will certainly not precede those who have fallen asleep. For the Lord himself will come down from heaven, with a loud command, with the voice of the archangel and with the trumpet call of God, and the dead in Christ will rise first. After that, we who are still alive and are left will be caught up together with them in the clouds to meet the Lord in the air. And so we will be with the Lord forever. Therefore encourage each other with these words" (1 Thessalonians 4:13-18).

Lori

Dashing Through the Snow

I watched videos at a friend's house late into the night one time. Stupid thing to do on a weeknight in the winter.

I think we watched three flicks and decided to quit about 3:00 a.m. Earlier in the evening there was about an inch of snow on the ground outside. By 3:00 in the morning the inch had become 12 inches.

No problem, I thought. *My CRX is the best little snow car in the West. It's gotten me through a midnight snowstorm in the Nevada desert* (that's another tale), *so it will get me out of this subdivision and onto the highway.*

But as the bottom of the car dragged through the snow, I had trouble moving forward at all. When I came to a four-way stop, I could choose the quick way on a road that had not been plowed or the long way on one that was already cleared. Guess which one I took.

About 300 yards from the stop sign I became stuck.

With the heater blasting, I got out of the car and looked around. Across the open fields, the wind blew clouds of snow from the surface and whipped them upward. At 3:30 a.m. I was stuck in the middle of the road with a tiny folding shovel and no coat. I hated to admit defeat, but I would just have to sit in the warm car and wait.

I had been standing there about 30 seconds when a pair of headlights appeared up on the main plowed road. A Chevy Blazer stopped, then reversed toward me through the snow. A man in a suit and tie got out.

"Need a pull?" he said. Taking a rope with a hook on each end, he pulled my CRX slowly back to the stop sign.

I asked him where he was going. Heading out to manage an inventory count at a grocery store, he said with a smile. I thanked him, and we drove off.

Coincidence? Luck? I don't know. I'll admit to you that I was not listening to God's voice during that year of my life. I was doing my own thing. So I didn't pray. But since that time God has gotten through to me. I know He takes care of my every move. He began even when I was ignoring Him. Why? Because He has a great plan for me.

He has one for you, too. You only have to stop doing your thing and let Him do His.

"Do not conform any longer to the pattern of this world, but be transformed by the renewing of your mind. Then you will be able to test and approve what God's will is—his good, pleasing and perfect will" (Romans 12:2).

Tim

Bedtime Story

I sat in his office and told him my problems. All of them. And I understood why people go to psychiatrists.

Two days before, I'd nervously dialed the college's Psychology Department. "Um, I'd like an appointment with Dr. Z."

"OK. Is this regarding a class you're taking from him?"

"No. I just wanted to talk to him about something," I stammered.

So, kindly, his student reader made an appointment. And kindly, Dr. Z, chair of the Psychology Department, kept the appointment.

"Dr. Z," I began after he invited me into his office, "I took General Psychology from you last year. And I need someone to talk to."

He listened.

"You see, I'm a college sophomore, and I don't think I'm ever going to sleep again. I haven't slept in four nights."

I guess I expected him to look shocked. To call the ambulance, to say I'd better quit school, to send me to a sanitarium in Switzerland.

But he didn't. He just listened, attentively, expressionless.

I repeated my point. "I haven't slept in *days.*" (When Alex Keaton couldn't sleep on an episode of *Family Ties,* I laughed. But when you haven't slept in 96 hours, you don't laugh; or you laugh at the wrong things.)

"Every night I go to bed and I just lie there. . . . Don't people go crazy if they don't sleep? Look at my bloodshot eyes. What's going to happen to me? I can't just not sleep." I laughed.

Dr. Z cleared his throat. Then he asked me about what was happening in my life. I told him about all the rough things—didn't even try to be optimistic or strong. In fact, I made things as bad as they seemed every night.

I'd just changed majors and had a heavy class load, including two speech classes. I had to come up with talks every other day and get up in front of people, and how could I concentrate if I didn't sleep? Laughter. My roommate had problems I felt I couldn't help her with, my dad had gotten a job transfer, my dog had died a few weeks ago, the dorm was noisy, my last haircut wasn't working, I was homesick, the deck monitor had pulled the perfume sample out of my magazine before I'd gotten the chance to smell it.

Not sleeping was the last straw. The final blow. I mean, what do you do when your days are bad and then they go on for 24 hours?

"I'm going to go crazy," I concluded. "My body needs sleep."

Dr. Z leaned forward and spoke kindly. "When your body reaches exhaustion, it will take sleep," he assured me.

Then he explained that students in high school and college have a lot of stress. Their schedules are extremely busy as they try to juggle school assignments, work, and social activities. Sleep gets sacrificed—sometimes by choice, sometimes not.

I listened and nodded.

"The last thing you need to do is worry about not sleeping, though," Dr. Z said. "Here's what you can do . . ." And he began to outline strategies, such as:

Pick an exercise you enjoy—swimming, biking, jogging—and do it regularly. Find ways to decrease your school, work, and social load. Take some time during each day to kick back and think. Enjoy healthy foods (and avoid caffeine).

Have a regular bedtime, and stick with it (studies show that you get your best sleep before midnight). In the same way, have a regular time to wake up (after nine hours, or more, if you need it). Establish a nightly routine before bedtime to "cue" your body: wash face, change clothes, listen to a song you like, talk to God. And reserve your bed for sleeping—avoid studying there or watching TV in bed.

Do what's morally right; nothing contributes better to a good night's sleep than a clear conscience. Place your life—all of it—in God's hands, remembering that He wants to give you the desires of your heart.

I left Dr. Z's office committed to trying his strategies. I did.

And I slept.

"Come to me, all you who are weary and burdened, and I will give you rest" (Matthew 11:28).

Lori

"Not That There's Anything Wrong With It"

At the public school I went to for a while, it was hip to be concerned about social problems. For instance, if you weren't against apartheid, you were super-weird. If you weren't tolerant of the gay lifestyle, you were prejudiced. Nobody at that school could tolerate intolerant people.

It's difficult to wade through that scene if these trendy social poses don't agree with your beliefs. Some issues are fairly easy to deal with. Some, like abortion, are not. And if your friends are all looking at you, you're squirming.

I've heard people complain that it took Adventists a long time to get involved in social issues. The church kept on preaching the same way it always had, while society's problems— AIDS, drug addiction, gangs, teen pregnancy, discrimination and prejudice, abortion—kept getting worse.

With the church's involvement in community service and its public stand on some issues, I think that Adventist attitudes are changing. But I see a danger in swinging too far toward a social issue orientation.

I've seen how social issues can become a religion of their own. That's what they are to secular people who see nothing in life beyond fixing the problems around them.

It's kind of bizarre to be accused by secular people of not taking care of society's problems. Our beliefs say that that's exactly what we're about. And we can't fault secular people who selflessly give time, talents, and money to help disadvantaged people. We find ourselves in a dilemma.

The way out is to know exactly what we believe and live it strongly. "'Love the Lord your God with all your heart and with all your soul and with all your mind.' This is the first and greatest commandment. And the second is like it: 'Love your neighbor as yourself'" (Matthew 22:37-39). Start from here, and no one will be able to accuse you of intolerance.

"The grace of God that brings salvation has appeared to all men. It teaches us to say 'No' to ungodliness and worldly passions, and to live self-controlled, upright and godly lives in this present age, while we wait for the blessed hope" (Titus 2:11-13)

Tim

23
Fading Fast

*T*hud.
I knew my job shadowing experience wasn't going very well. I felt like my stomach had just been punched—from the inside.
Pound. Pound. Pound.
Was that my heart? Yup. Uh-oh. Better retreat.
Blackout.
Now!
"Excuse me," I whispered to the emergency room doctor I was following around. He was fading from my sight fast.
He turned from the sutures he was putting into a woman's cut-

open palm. "Bend over," Dr. Regester commanded, standing and approaching me. "Put your head down."

The next thing I knew, I was out in the hospital hallway bent over, head down by my knees. "Take big, deep breaths," Dr. Regester instructed before he disappeared back into the emergency room.

When I got home that evening, I told my parents I didn't know if I should be a doctor after all. Or a nurse.

Of course, Dr. Regester was encouraging. He told me lots of doctors and nurses fainted at the sight of blood at first. That didn't mean anything. Now they perform open-heart surgery without a qualm.

Still, I couldn't ignore the nagging feeling that maybe I should look at a different career. I was still in academy, so I didn't have to decide just yet.

Then I got into college and signed up for my major. Nursing. But again I had a hard time ignoring the fact that I felt nauseous every time I entered the formaldehyde-scented anatomy and physiology lab. And I loved the times I could roam among musty books in the classics section of the library.

Finally I talked to my dad about it.

"Study what you enjoy and what you do best in," he said.

"But what can you do with an English major?" I wailed. "I'll never find a job."

"The Lord has given you talents and interests in a certain area, and He'll find a place for you when you've graduated," Dad assured me. "Don't worry. Change your major."

So I did. And I suddenly felt peace.

I know some of you worry about what career to choose. Let me give you the good advice I got. Go with your interests and talents. And let God take care of the rest. It works.

"Trust in the Lord with all your heart and lean not on your own understanding; in all your ways acknowledge him, and he will make your paths straight" (Proverbs 3:5, 6).

Lori

"Run Away!"

I worked in the back of the college bookstore while I was a student. Sometimes my friends would drop by and chat while I unpacked books.

One day my friend Mike* walked in and started joking around. I don't remember what we were talking about, but he was cussing up a storm. And I didn't try to tell him to stop. We both figured no one was around anyway.

Far away beyond the warehouse shelves sat my boss, the textbook manager. I thought she had left for the afternoon, but she was sitting quietly at her desk, and she couldn't help overhearing Mike's language.

He left, and she came over to me. Boy, was she upset! I couldn't say anything to defend him, so I said nothing.

I think we all get caught in this trap. We show our real selves when there are no teachers or bosses or 'rents or youth leader around—you know, all the cussing and bad jokes and gossiping and griping. If we do this hiding act often enough, we may end up thinking God is someone we can or should hide from.

But when Solomon said, "God will bring every act to judgment, everything which is hidden, whether it is good or evil" (Ecclesiastes 12:14, NASB), he wasn't just passing on a vague threat from God. He was saying that since we all have to face our real selves in God's presence one day, we should think about who we are and make sure God would approve. Some of us will have more than a red face on that judgment day.

"It is written, 'As surely as I live,' says the Lord, 'every knee will bow before me; every tongue will confess to God.' So then, each of us will give an account of himself to God" (Romans 14:11, 12).

Tim

---
* Not his real name.

48

Code Red

I've never gotten a traffic ticket. This does not mean I don't sometimes go 40 miles per hour in school zones, coast past stop signs, and drive through some very yellow lights.

But one of the first things I learned when I got my driving permit was how to evade the police. Even before practicing putting gas in the car's tank (and after learning where the radio was), I knew speed traps, where police officers ate lunch, and how to spot police cars under all environmental conditions. (For example, the police vehicles in our town had headlights sitting slightly farther apart than on most cars. After fixing that distance in my brain, I could usually detect them after dark.)

Few of my friends made it through high school dates and cruising without a traffic record. But I did.

Then a few weeks ago I got caught. I was driving home from . . . uhum, the Department of Motor Vehicles. I had been renewing my driver's license.

It was a sunny day, and the one-lane road home is curvy and sparsely traveled. Perfect. I cranked open the sunroof, turned on the radio unhealthfully loud, and drove unhealthfully fast.

I was having a wonderful time until a slow pickup truck suddenly backed out of a driveway and pulled in front of me. I pounced on the brakes and horn.

Because of the curves, I knew I couldn't pass safely. But to make sure the driver knew how seriously he had ruined my momentum, I drove alongside him on the wrong side of the road. At every curve I pulled in behind him and demonstrated the word "tailgating."

Just as I was pulling to his side again, I happened to look in my rearview mirror. A car had come up behind me—a kind of car I recognized. It had something too red and too circular on its roof. I cringed. Then the red and circular thing started flashing.

I pulled over obediently. I had had it. I knew it. This had probably been my worst driving, and he had been watching.

The police officer approached me cautiously and asked for my license. He studied it a moment.

"I pulled you over for several reasons," he said. "You were going 35 through town, and you were tailgating and driving on the wrong side of the road."

"I know. I'm sorry. I wasn't watching my speedometer." I had heard it's best to be agreeable. Crying came next.

"Where are you going?"

"I'm on my way home from the DMV. You won't believe this, but I just took my driving test and didn't miss any questions!" Reaching over to the seat beside me, I picked up my copy of the test and handed it to him as proof.

He scanned it, then asked, a little less gruffly, "Did the test say anything about speeding?"

"Yes. And as a matter of fact, I got that question right."

He paused, then handed the test back. "I'm going to let you go." He added paternally, "You better slow down in the future."

As I pulled away (very carefully) I realized that I still had a clean driving record. But I really didn't deserve it. It wasn't because I was a good driver. Just a bit of grace.

"It is by grace you have been saved, through faith—and this not from yourselves, it is the gift of God—not by works, so that no one can boast" (Ephesians 2:8, 9).

Lori

Do Clothes Make the Person?

I'm a scragger-muffin, rag-bucket kind of person. I deny it to myself and others. But no matter how much my friends have influenced me to dress nicely, decorate my office tastefully, keep my house neat and trendy and sophisticated—the real me keeps sprouting through.

I dated a very nice girl in college who applied her intelligence to the way she dressed (as well as to other areas of her life). Her credit card bill had a ripple effect on Wall Street, but without doubt her clothes were becoming, tasteful, and the best quality available.

Her rigorous standards rubbed off on me, and I began to take some care when I bought clothes. And I learned that the most expensive fad clothes and the cheapest clothes will often last the least amount of time.

I wouldn't have worried about my standard of clothes or anything else about my appearance if I could have avoided peer pressure. But peer pressure starts when we're very young and stays through life. We cannot escape it. Whether it's from friends, classmates, brothers and sisters and their friends, TV and movie characters, magazine advertisements, hot singers and musicians, parents, teachers, pastors, workmates, and, if we go on to college, professors and students around us—we're strongly influenced by what they're doing and what they expect of us.

Jesus said, "And why do you worry about clothes? See how the lilies of the field grow. They do not labor or spin. . . .

"Do not worry, saying, 'What shall we eat?' or 'What shall we drink?' or 'What shall we wear?' For the pagans [read "non-Christians"] run after all these things, and your heavenly Father knows that you need them" (Matthew 6:28-32).

Jesus gives us permission to be individuals. He encourages us to trust that our Father God will keep us from being embarrassed by our clothes or anything else in our circumstances.

This is not the same as saying "I don't care what anyone else thinks. I'm going to be me." Instead, we learn to be independent of others but completely dependent on God. And subsequently we find that He *does* keep His promise to meet our needs.

"Your beauty should not come from outward adornment. . . . Instead, it should be that of your inner self, the unfading beauty of a gentle and quiet spirit, which is of great worth in God's sight" *(1 Peter 3:3, 4).*

Tim

27
Fairy Tale?

Sebastian Flyte is a 19-year-old kid. He tows around a teddy bear and asks childlike questions.

One afternoon Sebastian and his friend Charles are sitting in the sun. Charles, who believes that Christianity is a myth, questions Sebastian about his faith.

"I suppose they try to make you believe an awful lot of nonsense?" Charles says.

"Is it nonsense? I wish it were. It sometimes sounds terribly sensible to me," Sebastian responds.

"But my dear Sebastian, you can't seriously *believe* it all."

"Can't I?"

"I mean about Christmas and the star and the three kings and the ox and the ass."

"Oh yes. I believe that. It's a lovely idea."

"But you can't *believe* things because they're lovely ideas."

"But I *do*. That's how I believe."

Sebastian is a character in the book *Brideshead Revisited*. And he is an endearing character because he refuses to grow up. While all the people around him are becoming pessimistic and cynical, he shows innocence, belief, optimism, and childhood.

Remember when you believed an idea simply because you liked the sound of it? Never mind proof, facts, and statistics. It sounded *nice,* and you were drawn to the niceness. You liked the idea of a guardian angel with you always and Jesus hearing and answering your prayers (even when you didn't close your eyes).

Sebastian's like that. And people like him for it. Of course, they don't always think he's wise in his belief. We learn in growing up that blind faith is handicapped. We should have *reasons* for accepting and believing things. Just because something is lovely doesn't mean it's true.

But we tend to forget something very important: sometimes lovely ideas *are* true. Like the Christmas story, and heaven, and God's love.

And rejecting ideas because they are lovely isn't any wiser—maybe it's less wise—than accepting them on those grounds. We've all met people who discount every nice concept as unreal romanticism, who find tragic stories more believable than happy ones, who, in their shivering demand for cold proof, grow out of God, faith, and wonder.

But that's not Christian maturity. As we grow we can (and should) search for reasons for belief. We look at the historical facts of Christ's time on earth. We consider the Bible and the personal experiences of people around us.

And maybe we also ought to take into account our built-in ability to believe in what we haven't seen, our human compulsion to dream and imagine, and our childlike attraction to lovely ideas. These too can be reasons for believing in God.

We don't have to lose innocence, belief, optimism, and childlikeness in order to grow up. In fact, right now most of us could stand a fairy-tale glimpse of heaven. A talk with God. A stubborn confidence that goodness is really stronger than badness.

The idea of Christianity is lovely indeed. *And* true.

"Let the little children come to me, and do not hinder them, for the kingdom of God belongs to such as these. I tell you the truth,

anyone who will not receive the kingdom of God like a little child will never enter it" (Mark 10:14, 15).

Lori

Don't Bother Me

My best friend in college, Tracy,* was a pretty strong Christian. She (yes, *she*—but not a girlfriend) had started down the path toward God and was gung ho about Him. I was not interested at all.

After we left college we talked on the phone now and then. Tracy would mention God, and it really bothered me. She'd say something like "I've learned to open up to God so much lately," and I'd be going, "Uh-huh." *Let's talk about anything else.*

Why did it bother me? For one thing, I wasn't at the same point in my spiritual journey as she was. I hadn't even started mine, really. And I didn't want to hear about this subject I wanted to avoid.

Tracy kept encouraging me to give God a try. I kept saying "Maybe," but I meant no.

You might wonder who was the one doing wrong in this situation. At that time I thought she was being inconsiderate. Shouldn't she have kept quiet if I seemed uncomfortable? Was she forcing God down my throat?

Of course, I was pushing away the Holy Spirit. And Tracy was probably asking the Holy Spirit to guide her and to talk to me.

She was still acting like my best friend in every other way, so I couldn't say she had pushed this on me without being a good friend first. She kept bringing God into our friendship because she couldn't keep Him out.

I stayed away from God for a couple more years. But gradually His Spirit's voice began to get through to me. Although I can't say

54

Tracy directly persuaded me, the thoughts she had planted in my head stopped annoying me and became welcome. I wanted to talk about the same things she did.

I'm glad my friend never wavered, never hid her happiness or her faith. She never apologized or backed down, but trusted our friendship to God.

Whether you are taking steps toward God or avoiding Him, I can tell you that I found a lot of happiness and relief when God and I became friends. And even though I kind of resisted at first, I decided quickly that avoiding happiness was pointless. Now I say, "Go ahead and have all you want."

"Praise the Lord, O my soul, and forget not all his benefits—who forgives all your sins and heals all your diseases, who redeems your life from the pit and crowns you with love and compassion, who satisfies your desires with good things" (Psalm 103:2-5,

---

* Not her real name. It's her sister's name.

Take Me Home

I never ran away from home when I was little. I knew I would get hopelessly homesick and come running back. It's anticlimactic to wander up the driveway at sunset asking for dinner.

But when it came time to go away to college I was ready. I was an adult, 18 years of age, and I would be just fine, thank you. I mean, I would have to be. You have to grow up sometime.

Of course, I did what most other kids leaving home do—I took as much of home as possible with me. At least I limited myself to one carful of home. Some people I knew rented U-Haul trailers or even trucks and moved tables, curtains, waterbeds, life-size teddy bears, and fish tanks with them to school.

After I distributed my possessions about the dorm room, I thought things would be quite nice. But when Mom and Dad drove off, home suddenly seemed very, very far away.

I was going to be strong and grown-up, though. And so that first year away from home I exuded strength and independence, walked around smiling, and spent lots of nights crying into my pillow.

Then I discovered that my roommates were homesick too. And so were at least half the girls on the hall. And the guys. And even teachers. It seemed that everyone was homesick for somebody or something.

After all, the word "home" stands for all that is familiar, comfortable, warm, and valuable to you. You can feel homesick for a specific place, a person, an object, a feeling, or a relationship.

That's when I began trying some strategies. First, I looked at the positive side of homesickness. If I was feeling homesick, I obviously had some things to be thankful for. After all, we usually miss what is good.

So when I felt down, I began concentrating on how lucky I was to have a family I wanted to be near rather than one I couldn't wait to get away from. I tried to focus on the good friendships I'd made and places that had become special to me.

Next I tried to identify the special qualities of home I missed most. Maybe it was my dad's good listening, family worship, or the smell of chocolate-chip cookies. Then I tried to create some of home right where I was, for myself and for the other homesick sufferers around me (whether they admitted it or not!). I tried to be a good listener like Dad, got involved in a worship group , and baked some cookies.

Most of all I reminded myself that Jesus knows all about homesickness. When I felt that loneliness come on, I talked to Him, resting in the assurance that He loved me enough to leave His own home so I could live there with Him someday.

"Father, I want those you have given me to be with me where I am, and to see my glory, the glory you have given me because you

loved me before the creation of the world" (John 17:24).

Threat of Arrest

I received a huge packet in the mail one day with the official stamp of the state of Georgia on it. Inside was a summons (a threat, basically) that unless I appeared in court in Savannah, Georgia, on such-and-such a day, I could be arrested the next time I set foot on Georgia soil.

Why should I be arrested in Georgia? I wondered. *What terrible deed have I committed that I can't recall?*

The memory trickled back. My brother and I had driven to Savannah one weekend because it was the closest beach to our college—only six hours' drive. We drove all night, slept a little in the morning, and then headed to the beach.

I found a place near the beach to park the car. You know those little roads off the main drag that dead-end into the sand dunes. Locking the old Nova, we cruised down to the waves.

As we piled in the car later that day, I noticed a faint white line on one side of the car. *Hmm, must be a parking place outline.* Then I saw the ticket under the windshield wiper.

I looked around for a sign forbidding parking and saw none. Finally I noticed that the overgrown, drooping shrub next to my parking spot was covering up a dusty old parking meter.

Feeling cheated, I pushed the ticket under the seat and forgot about it for two months. The big manila envelope brought it all back.

Since I couldn't go to Savannah for fear of arrest and perhaps execution, I took the other option listed in the summons: paying the fine. For the luxury of waiting two months to pay my debt to society, I now owed $27 instead of the $9.75 on the original ticket or the $3 meter charge.

You know what I'm thinking here. Your sins will find you out. Pay attention to the rules. Blah blah blah. The threat of arrest and a $27 fine reminded me that the rules are not going away, no matter how upset I am with them. Life is a whole lot happier (and cheaper) if you're not fighting the rules.

I got stung by a jellyfish twice that day at the beach near Savannah. I've never been back. I know when I'm not wanted.

"I have chosen the way of truth; I have set my heart on your laws. I hold fast to your statutes, O Lord; do not let me be put to shame" (Psalm 119:30, 31).

Tim

It Doesn't Add Up

The past few days I've been thinking about irony. Check out these ironies:

- Kurt Cobain felt so hopeless that he committed suicide. The name of his band was Nirvana (a word often used to mean "bliss").

- My friend was telling me that her 3-year-old didn't want to go to bed the other night. When she said he had to, he got so mad that he hit her. Wanting her kid to *unlearn* that response real quick, she put him over her knee and spanked him, all the while saying, "Don't you ever hit anyone again!" She had to stop herself from laughing out loud as she realized what was happening!

- Jesus said that by giving up the things we cling to in life, we will actually gain peace and happiness (see Matthew 10:39).

58

- When we get insulted and teased and persecuted because of our faith, we should rejoice (see Matthew 5:11).

I've also been thinking about God's math. I was never good in math, so I'm not surprised that I'm confused at some of God's figuring. But one thing's clear—we humans always come out on the good end. We're always the winners in any transactions we do with God. Try these:

- With five loaves and two fish Jesus fed more than 5,000 people (see Mark 6:30-44).
- When we get together with another person to talk about or to Jesus, He's there in our presence (see Matthew 18:20).
- When we help poor, hurting people around us, God counts that as if we're doing it for Him (see Matthew 25:40).
- One death (Jesus') saves us all.

I don't know about you, but those things don't add up to me. I'm just glad that when God does the math (and plans the ironies), I always come out better than if I had done it myself. Maybe I should turn over my calculator and calendar to Him.

"You know the grace of our Lord Jesus Christ, that though he was rich, yet for your sakes he became poor, so that you through his poverty might become rich" (2 Corinthians 8:9).

Lori

Forget Warp Speed

After five years at an Adventist college, I went to a public university in California for grad school. My English friend Tim lived in the coed dorms, while I lived in an apartment. We bought a TV together and kept it in his room.

At 10:30 almost every weeknight we'd watch *Star Trek* reruns together. We were trying to discover whether the dating system in *Star Trek* actually meant anything. (This does nothing for your academic or spiritual life, but I didn't notice back then.)

Our *Star Trek* ritual had a beneficial result. Tim's next-door neighbors in the dorm, Lisa and Linda, came over to watch with us sometimes. After a while Lisa stopped coming, but Linda dropped by more and more often.

Star Trek visits turned into yakking sessions, the three of us comparing our varied backgrounds.

One evening I said, "I've been wanting to try skiing in the San Bernardino Mountains."

Linda immediately replied, "Me too."

So I said, "When shall we go?"

There it was—our first date.

I thought Linda had no idea I'd been thinking of asking her out. Later she revealed that she'd kept coming to *Star Trek* in the hope that I would get around to it.

After another month or two of getting to know Linda, I realized that she was the one for my future. We dated for two and a half years, and every day I became more sure.

I found that if you really enjoy a special person's presence, you don't mind spending months and months getting to know her or him very well in order to be absolutely sure. No matter how much you love someone, waiting for the right time never hurts a loving relationship.

"For this reason a man will leave his father and mother and be united to his wife, and the two will become one flesh." "So they are no longer two, but one. Therefore what God has joined together, let man not separate" (Matthew 19:5, 6).

Tim

A Visit With the Gods

We gasped a lot that morning. First when we drove around the modern city of Athens and saw, far above every high-rise, the ancient ruins on the Acropolis. Then when we got stuck in a traffic circle and watched 10 cars converging on us while 20 horns beeped.

We gasped as we got to Omonoia Square for the fourth time when all we wanted to do was get to the Acropolis.

"Oh, it's over to our right now."

"Isn't that the Acropolis behind us? Shouldn't we be going that way?"

"If we pass the Parliament building one more time, that guard is going to think I'm flirting with him."

My family had dreamed of visiting Greece for many years. And here we were, lost in Athens. But never out of sight of the impressive Temple of Athena high on the rocky hill they call the Acropolis.

Finally our rented Golf stopped beneath that hill. We gasped again when we had to pay $5 apiece to mount the crowded stairs up to the temples.

When we reached the top and tried to fit it all into our camera lens, we gasped once more. Our eyes followed the columns up and up to the sculpted gods at the top, who'd been basking in their ornate entablatures since the 500s B.C.

We were reprimanded for standing too near the sculptures in the Acropolis museum. And when I tried to take a picture of a handsome French artist next to a marble Aphrodite, the museum guard gave us both a lecture on the sacredness of the place and the antiquities. "You are not in your living room!" he shouted.

We listened to a tour guide talk about the Parthenon, the large marble temple built to the goddess Athena, and the smaller temple of Athena Nike. She explained that the ancient Greeks had many gods.

These gods were like humans, with all the passions and desires of men and women. They got very angry, often drank or ate too much, let sexual desires control them, and were greedy, undisciplined, and arrogant. Greek gods fought each other for supremacy and power. The basic difference between humans and gods was that the gods were immortal, powerful, and eternally young.

Dusty, hot, and sore, we descended from the high place of the Greek gods. Through the thick Athens smog we saw Mars Hill to our right. The hill where the early Christian apostle Paul stood and tried to tell the people about the God he knew. The God so different from theirs.

We weaved into Omonoia Square for the sixth time, down Stadiou Street, and finally found the Herodian Hotel, where we were staying.

My father pulled into the parking garage on Amalias Avenue. It was a back street, but cars sped by even there. As a bus screeched through, my mother pulled us off the road. And then in the brief lull between cars, we saw the cat.

It made us gasp, more than we'd gasped all morning. For it was a small cat, and its back was broken.

Using its two functioning front legs, the animal dragged itself from behind the tire of a parked car and into the street. Through its brown and gold fur we could see the jut mark, just past its front legs. There its backbone dropped toward the ground, leaving more than half its body useless and paralyzed.

We watched, horrified, as it hopped and pulled its body. Its lifeless tail and back legs swept along the dirty street behind it. It turned its head back every few seconds, frightened green eyes checking for another object such as the one that had done this to it.

"We have to do something!" we cried, our stomachs sick.

"Is there a humane society? A Society for Prevention of Cruelty to Animals?"

People passed by as if they didn't notice the dying animal.

I ran to a man turning the corner. "There's a cat. . ." I began.

He looked blank.

My mother came up behind me. "Meow, meow," she tried to explain.

He smiled, then laughed. "He thinks it's funny!" I cried.

"He doesn't understand," my mother said. She pointed to the cat down the street.

He craned his neck, then shrugged.

"Let's check with the hotel," my dad said decisively. "Maybe they can tell us where a Red Cross is. At least they'll understand English."

We ran inside. The man at the desk appeared unconcerned, but he gave us directions to the Red Cross. "I don't know if they're open on Sunday," he added.

But we had to try. We dashed outside to the cat. It wasn't in the street anymore. We ran and looked under every car on the street. It was nowhere. We looked in the alley, opened the gate leading into a deserted yard. We had lost our dying cat.

We hoped its mother found it or someone else picked it up and took it to help, if it could be helped anymore. But we never knew.

That evening we'd planned to go the much-advertised Sound and Light Show at the Acropolis. We were pretty solemn on the way there.

As we sat in the folding chairs on the grassy hill and watched red, then yellow, then green lights cut through the columns of the temple, the pain in that cat's eyes came back to us.

And the voices of the actors playing the Greek gods sounded pretty hollow passing through that mighty structure. The passionate Greek chorus over the loudspeaker was tinny and cold.

And I thought that I do not need gods high on a hill that I can see from every spot in the city. I do not need the beautiful stone figures preserved through ages.

What I need is a God who is not too proud or too busy to come down to Amalias Avenue, to where a cat and I hurt. I want a God who understands my pain, who stubbed His toes on ancient stones, felt the dust and the heat, and the hurt of a broken bone.

I want a God better than me—great enough to save me from sin. But a God who cares about my everyday problems.

I want such a God. And I have such a God.

"Not one sparrow, worth only half a penny, can fall to the ground without your Father knowing it. And the very hairs of your head are all numbered. So don't be afraid; you are more valuable to him than a whole flock of sparrows" (Matthew 10:29-31, NLT).

Lori

You're the *Mona Lisa*

Let's just say you're a Rembrandt painting. Or you're a Michelangelo ceiling. Maybe you're a rare Chinese vase.

Over time, you've deteriorated. You look kind of ratty—molded over, crusty, covered up with dirt. No one recognizes your true value anymore. At least, not by looking at you.

But some museum curator decides to restore you. Someone who knows how to apply chemicals that bleach out the dirt and, at the same time, restore your dazzling colors. You go from garage-sale skankiness to National Museum of Art finery.

This is what Jesus does for our souls. God says that our righteousness is like abhorrent, stinky rags (see Isaiah 64:6), and He's not kidding. But we don't have to stay that way.

God knows that we have eternal, limitless value. He can see it under all the garbage. But most people around us can't. Sometimes we can't even see it in ourselves. Jesus took the chance on dying for each of us because He knew what He'd find under the dirt.

"O Lord, you are our Father. We are the clay, you are the potter; we are all the work of your hand" (Isaiah 64:8). Tim

Blood on the Ceiling

I was sitting there at a red light. Just listening to some tunes and waiting for green.

Suddenly, *crash!*

The next thing I knew, the paramedics were taping my forehead to a board. Next they strapped my back onto the board and carefully shifted me onto a stretcher.

Then I was inside the ambulance.

"I'm not paralyzed, am I?" I asked. (Yeah, I grew up hearing the story of Joni Eareckson Tada too.)

"Just stay still," someone instructed.

"But I can move my toes." I wiggled them to emphasize my point.

"You just relax," came the reply.

Relax?

"How could I move my toes if I'm paralyzed?" I persisted.

"Only about half the people who have spinal cord injuries have instant paralysis," the paramedic rattled off. "The rest have suffered an injury, and when they move, they sever their spinal cord. That's why we're taking precautions with you. So don't move."

I didn't.

When we pulled up to Riverside General Hospital, an emergency nurse yanked open the doors. "Is this from the accident on Van Buren with the horse?" came her voice. "How's the horse?"

The horse? What about me?

Evidently a man in a van pulling a horse trailer had seen the line of stopped cars at the red light, but he was too drunk to find the brake. Instead he hit the gas pedal, plowing into four cars (including mine) at 60 miles per hour.

They wheeled me into the emergency room "holding tank"—I wasn't a "life and death" situation, just a possible quadriplegic. They made one phone call for me—to my roommate, who wasn't home (my parents lived eight hours away). The ER staff were too busy to try anyone else.

So for three hours I waited alone. Strapped to that board, able only to look up. At a dirty, bloodstained ceiling.

Once in a while an aide would come in and take my blood pressure. "It's my first day," he explained. (I couldn't turn to see his face—I knew only his voice.) He pumped the band up pretty tight a few times. It hurt.

But you know what? I actually liked the pain. 'Cause I knew I could still feel.

During those three hours waiting for a doctor to see me, I talked to Jesus a lot. More than I'd ever talked to Him before. And I felt Him sticking tight beside me—closer than I'd ever felt Him before.

He even helped me come to grips with the fact that my life might change a whole lot. When the X-rays came back and I found out I'd be OK, I was happy. Oh, yeah, definitely. But right then I was OK with whatever happened.

Strange. I can't explain it, but I have a feeling you'll know what I mean someday—if you don't already. When everybody and everything you depend on falls out from beneath you, Someone still holds you.

Looking up isn't a bad idea.

"Do not fear, for I am with you; do not be dismayed, for I am your God. I will strengthen you and help you; I will uphold you with my righteous right hand" (Isaiah 41:10).

Lori

Agreeable Disagreeing

I was once asked the question How do you deal with people who demand that you agree with their opinion on a social issue?

Here's my answer: If you disagree with another person's view, say so politely and tactfully.

This is great in theory, but I haven't put it into practice much, so let's try a scenario and test it.

Let's say a student at your school says in class that legalizing mind-altering drugs like cocaine and heroin would solve the drug problems in this country. Other kids in the room argue in favor of the idea because (a) they could then try out the drugs themselves, (b) they wouldn't get jailed for getting caught, (c) they predict less violence connected with drug use, and (d) the drugs would cost less.

You yourself have already rejected drug use of any kind as damaging to your body and mind, but right now you may like the idea of keeping quiet. This issue should be left to each person's individual choice, right?

Let's say that someone who knows you're a Christian asks what you think. Now you have to answer.

As I said above, the first rule is Be polite. Nothing betrays the real motives of some vehement anti-abortion protesters, for instance, like rudeness. So whether you feel passionate or just defensive about your belief, don't let others around you pull you away from courtesy.

Concerning the second rule, being tactful involves disagreeing without putting the other person down. We often respond to an idea we disagree with by saying "That's stupid because . . ." or "I think that's wrong." With that we imply that the person is stupid. Concentrate on the subject, and keep the other person's feelings in mind, even if you think their beliefs are morally wrong.

Remember that only with God are all things (including successful debates) possible.

"But I tell you: Love your enemies and pray for those who persecute you, that you may be [sons and daughters] of your Father in heaven" (Matthew 5:44, 45).

Tim

Lady and the Equestrian Will

Jordan Hollow Horse Farm was an unlikely place for my sister and me to be vacationing.

First, we're both scared of horses. Second, you have to understand that we grew up in the suburbs.

When our family visits the Everglades, Teri and I exclaim, "Wow, this smells like it does in the Pirates of the Caribbean ride at Disneyland!" When we see waving fields of wheat, we say, "How pretty! It looks like the wallpaper in the dentist's office."

But this was our first vacation together—just the two of us, without Mom and Dad. Teri had come to Maryland to visit me, and we were determined to do something exotic, *different.*

We began at the travel agency, browsing the racks of brochures. But when the woman gave us price breakdowns for the Bahamas cruise, we had to say, "Oh, thank you—we were just wondering."

Then while reading a brochure about the Shenandoah Valley, Teri came across an advertisement and a very blurry picture of a 200-year-old horse farm. It advertised "lovely rooms, cozy conversations and quiet games, walks on the farm, swimming, porch sitting, interesting people . . ."

Well, it would be different. And we wanted different.

So the next morning we found ourselves driving through the stone gate of Jordan Hollow Farm. When we saw the green rolling hills, shade trees, and shiny horses grazing, we felt enchanted.

The owner's wife, Marley Beers, showed us to our room above the corral. We smiled at the gingham bedspreads, fresh flowers on the table, and a hand-embroidered doily on the nightstand.

"Where's the pool?" we asked.

"There's a lake about a mile from here," she responded. "But you girls really ought to go horseback riding."

We looked at each other.

"There's a ride for beginners in a few minutes. Jody's real good with the horses."

So we found ourselves down at the stables waiting with the other nervous beginners, mostly lawyers and businesspeople from Washington, D.C.

And then a girl with a ponytail and bowed legs strode in. She was wearing a tank top, jeans, and cowboy boots. Somehow we knew she was Jody.

"All right, first thing. Everyone needs to wear one of these," she announced, holding up an equestrian helmet.

"Why?" someone asked.

"Policy." Jody pointed to a sign above the rack of helmets: "All Riders Must Wear Hard Hats."

Teri and I wanted to go back to our room right about then. But we followed the others and put hats on. We tried to be brave and ignore the fact that we'd just curled our hair to take pictures of ourselves on horses.

Jody took care of that problem, though. "No cameras!" she yelled.

We heard a chorus of moans, then a pile of Nikons, Pentaxes, and Canons appeared in the hay.

Jody clopped out to the corral, and somehow we knew we were supposed to follow her. Out there she motioned to us one at a time, and matched us with a horse.

Teri was glad to get an old spotted horse named Hallie. "At least he won't go fast," she whispered.

Jody pointed at me and then a tall brown horse.

"I really haven't ridden much," I hesitated. "Is he fast? I'd rather have an old one."

"She's pregnant," Jody said, giving me a shove onto the horse named Lady.

And then we were on the open trail. We climbed a hill and passed by a mountain lake trimmed with wild mustard. We listened to the clop of the horses on the road and looked at the blue-mountained skyline and the cloud-brushed air.

Normally we would have raced over this road, car windows rolled up, the radio blaring. Today we were part of the scenery.

Then we entered a wooded trail. And the problems began.

Hallie tailgated the horse in front of Teri. The horse swished its tail, and Hallie reared.

"Tell her *Ho!*" Jody yelled to Teri.

Then my Lady began to eat the foliage along the trail.

"Pull her away!" Jody ordered. "Make her move. Kick her sides!"

"But she's pregnant."

"Kick her!"

Exasperated, I did. Lady took off running.

"Stop her!" Jody screamed after me.

"How?" I yelled back.

"Why don't you push the off button?" Jody snarled, riding up and taking Lady's reins.

After that I felt determined to establish a relationship with my horse. We were going to get along. She was going to obey me. Like my Honda. Like my computer.

But Lady wasn't at all like them. Most of the time she obeyed. But sometimes she didn't. And always I had the uneasy feeling of dealing with a separate will. Ultimately, she could walk wherever she wanted—no matter what I said.

That got me thinking about God and the freedom He gives us.

Originally everything was perfect. Harmonic.

Renaissance philosophers wrote about "the music of the spheres." They believed that as the planets revolve, each gives out a different note. This results in heavenly music that can occur only when there is perfect harmony in the universe, when every planet is moving in accord with heaven, every being on every planet saying yes.

70

And then the first no sounded through the heavens. Like a violin string breaking.

It must have pained the ears of a God of order and harmony. And He could have prevented it—if He'd built in control keys. If, instead of horses, He'd made Hondas; instead of people, computers.

But the funny thing is I seldom think about my car or my computer. And I sometimes wonder how Lady is doing—if her colt was born OK, if she's still stopping to eat the foliage.

And if I ever get back to Jordan Hollow Farm, I wouldn't think of riding any other horse. Because Lady and I made it back to the corral after struggling to harmonize our wills. And that builds a relationship you can't get any other way.

"Now the Lord is the Spirit, and where the Spirit of the Lord is, there is freedom" (2 Corinthians 3:17).

Lori

How to Prevent Divorce

Some of my friends grew up in a home in which a divorce happened. The family split up, parents got remarried, and the children were hit with the psychological equivalent of a baseball bat to the head. The scars last a lifetime.

You've heard the old saying that an ounce of prevention is worth a pound of cure. So maybe it's time to consider a few grams of divorce prevention.

In my opinion, prevention begins when you're a teenager. No matter what your home situation is now, you can take steps to have a happy, successful marriage yourself.

71

1. Begin thinking now about what you would expect from the person you will marry. Get some clues from the kind of friends you appreciate most. They're the people you have a lot in common with, right? The ones who stick by you and encourage you.

2. If or when you begin to date people, think consciously about the fact that you are looking for someone who suits you—who matches you or complements you. Say you meet Joe/Jennifer at the beginning of school, and ever after, when you pass him/her in the hall, your heart beats itself up. If you keep suitability in mind, you'll more likely be able to concentrate on getting to know what that special person is like instead of getting distracted by emotion and physical desire.

3. If you don't want to face the pain and disruption of divorce when you're older, make a pledge to yourself that you won't do anything to yourself or with others that might cause pain to the person you do end up marrying. Also, don't do anything that you wouldn't want your future husband or wife to have done themselves. Fair's fair.

4. As you get to the end of your teen years and maybe date someone seriously, take as much time as you think you need to be sure that you and your Sweet Pookie are really suited to each other. My wife, Linda, and I dated for two and a half years before we said "I do," even though both of us thought we had found the right person early on. Each of us wanted to know lots about the other—about our goals, our morals, our families, what we wanted in life. We wished to see how the other person handled difficulties and accomplished goals. It takes time.

You won't lose any fun in your social life by keeping in mind where you're going and what you're looking for. And you may save yourself and your children a lifetime of extreme pain.

"I tell you that anyone who divorces his wife, except for marital unfaithfulness, causes her to become an adulteress, and anyone who marries the divorced woman commits adultery" (Matthew 5:32).

Tim

Nevermore

I don't want to die. And when I talk about death I always end up saying ridiculous things like "I'm scared to death of death" or "I'm dying to be immortal."

It just doesn't sound very nice to be dead. Oh, I know it will be like sleeping. No pain. No worry. No sensations.

But I don't want to feel nothing. I want to know what's going on in the world, what the weather's going to be like tomorrow, if my auto mechanic will ever believe in God.

Life is exciting.

There's also something sacred about life. Something that makes you feel less lonely with even a fern or a goldfish in the room. Something that makes a puppy, even with vet bills and house training, nicer to have than a stuffed dog. Something that makes you feel silly for having conversations with a doll, but quite rational in having them with your hamster.

The breath of life. When it's there, we know the difference. Animate and inanimate.

Sometimes the line between life and death seems very close. People look at an autistic child, a paralyzed girl, a man in a prison camp, or a patient in a coma and say, "It would be better if that person would die."

Others don't agree. They know there's something soothing about warm skin and a heartbeat.

Perhaps my life hasn't been bad enough. Maybe I haven't felt *real* hunger, depression, exhaustion, or hopelessness. Maybe then I would welcome the idea of a long sleep. As it is, I like sleep primarily for how much better it makes me feel when I wake up.

I just can't get used to the concept of death. It doesn't seem right, and I don't want it to happen to me. So I live, desperately trying to avoid potentially death-causing situations. I don't skydive or race cars. I don't use saccharin or walk through alleys at night.

But avoiding life-threatening situations gets tiresome, and I have a feeling it cuts into my living.

Besides, it doesn't work. Once I sat in my car at a red light and got hit by a drunk driver. Another time I stepped into an elevator, pushed a button, and ended up in a dark basement. Life is life-threatening. It's the world we live in.

I don't like that, and I don't think God does either. He breathes life. Death was the consequence of sin and not part of His plan. But death had to become the price for life.

To us humans, the two are inseparable. Life, then death. One follows the other.

But God is going to turn that around. Life will be the final word—though we won't even have the concept of final.

John Donne ends the sonnet "Death, Be Not Proud" by saying, "Death, thou shalt die." That's what's going to happen in heaven.

The death of death.

"He will wipe every tear from their eyes. There will be no more death or mourning or crying or pain, for the old order of things has passed away" (Revelation 21:4).

Do You Have a Youth Group?

What's your youth group like? Do you even have one at your church?

Do you like it the way it is? Or could it be better?

Some teens don't like church because they have to be there. If they had a choice, they'd stay away. You may not feel that way, but someone in your group probably does. You can do something to make it a better experience for you and for others who feel forced to be there.

First, if you don't have a cool name, you could think one up. I heard about a youth group in Yakima, Washington, that calls itself Heart Rock Café. A group in Idaho named itself the Salt Company a few years back. I'm sure there are good ones I haven't heard about. When your group is together, get everyone's input and find a hot name.

The big plus about a name is that all of a sudden your group has a special identity. Older people in your church will give teens more respect because they'll feel as though they're up against a united force. And you'll feel good about going to the group on Sabbath.

Second, figure out what you're there for. Maybe all of you are there because you want to worship God. People who go to church for that reason usually enjoy it more than anyone else. But you can't force anyone to want to worship God. So maybe some of your group are just there to pass the time or see friends. It's a good idea to talk about it honestly and openly in the group so you can all get something good out of being there.

Third, think what you like to do in the group. If you like to sing, sing. You can sing for an hour if you want to. Take it from Ellen White, who said that singing praise is worship of God as much as any other kind of worship. You can talk about problems, study something in the Bible that bothers or mystifies you, or invite an outside speaker who could enlighten you. If you ask people to come and tell the group how they became a Christian and why they are one now, you'll get all sorts of weird stories. Everybody's got a story.

See you Sabbath.

"Where two or three come together in my name, there am I with them" (Matthew 18:20).

Tim

Good Public Relations

When I returned to the Pacific Union College dorm one afternoon, I found a message on the board: "Call Dr. Chase."

I dialed his number, wondering what the chair of the Communications Department wanted.

"Hello," he greeted me. "St. Helena Hospital has requested a public relations intern this quarter. I think you would be perfect." He explained that I would get practicum credit and asked, "Can you report to the director of public relations tomorrow?"

I agreed and the next afternoon found myself walking into Mr. Barnett's office in the basement of the hospital. He motioned for me to have a seat, and told me all about public relations and what he would like me to do during my time there.

He ended by saying, "I'm sorry we don't have an office for you. We'll set up a desk in the office of our director of publications, Kim Peckham."

Before I left, Mr. Barnett took me on a tour of the department. When he led me into Kim's office, I was surprised to see a handsome, friendly guy.

Hmmm, I thought. *This is going to be fun.*

As I spent time with Kim, a recent graduate of Union College, I grew to respect and like him more and more. Not only did I learn about public relations that quarter; I learned how easy it was to talk to him about good books and God's leading in people's lives.

When my internship ended we exchanged addresses, and I headed to La Sierra University for graduate study. The next two Christmases we exchanged cards, and then two years later Kim looked me up on a visit to southern California.

Over brunch at Lake Arrowhead we found ourselves remembering our conversations in the basement of St. Helena Hospital and sharing how God had led us since. And this time we didn't say good-bye for long—we found God leading us to jobs at the same place, and over the next few years we became best friends, fell in love, and married. (Ah!)

For years I'd prayed to God about my love life, including prayers for "the anonymous man I might someday marry." But it was hard to wait for God.

He brought Kim to my attention, though—the very last quarter of my senior year and in the basement of a hospital. Not exactly when and where I'd expected to meet the man of my dreams. But when God does things, they always turn out right.

If you trust Him with everything, including your love life, you're bound to find yourself far from the basement and close to the sun!

"Delight yourself in the Lord and he will give you the desires of your heart. . . . Be still before the Lord and wait patiently for him" (Psalm 37:4-7).

Lori

A Little Jewelry

Actually, I have a few jewels here. Put these sayings away some-where in your brain, and you can reach for them at the right moment someday.

● "You can't hold a man down without staying down with him."—Booker T. Washington.

● "I have been driven many times to my knees by the overwhelming conviction that I had nowhere else to go. My own wisdom, and that of all about me, seemed insufficient for the day."—Abraham Lincoln.

- "A smile is an inexpensive way to improve your looks."—Charles Gordy.
- "He that can have patience can have what he will."—Benjamin Franklin.
- "I have decided to stick with love. Hate is too great a burden to bear."—Martin Luther King, Jr.
- "There is nothing good for a man under the sun except to eat and to drink and to be merry."—Ecclesiastes 8:15, NASB.
- "The unexamined life is not worth living."—Socrates.
- "Eighty percent of success is showing up."—Woody Allen.
- "I've read the last page of the Bible. It's going to turn out all right."—Billy Graham.

"He who testifies to these things says, 'Yes, I am coming soon.' Amen. Come, Lord Jesus" (Revelation 22:20).

Teacher, Teacher

Before I became an editor, I went to grad school. And as part of my "education," I got assigned to teach freshman comp classes.

I'm sure I learned more by being a teacher than by being a student. Especially one evening.

I'd been teaching my college freshman logic and argumentation, as the textbook outlined. Suddenly I thought, *What better way to learn how to argue logically than to have a debate?*

So I divided the class into debate teams, helped them choose topics, and outlined the debate format. Then they were to research their topics.

Well, debate night came, and we were ready to begin when a distinguished African-American man entered the classroom and sat at the back. Dr. Briggs, my instructor. He'd told me he'd be visiting my classroom to observe my teaching.

The first debate team came forward. The topic: Should women be drafted into the military?

The first student on side 1 began speaking. And I began shifting in my seat. His arguments were models of faulty logic—*and* they were offending all the females in the room!

The second speaker did worse—if that's possible. And when it came time for side 2 to refute side 1's arguments, they laid into *them,* not their arguments.

"I could not understand what they were saying," one student complained, shaking his head.

"They cannot speak proper English and do not know about women," another commented.

Uh-oh. Maybe this wasn't such a good idea. As the evening wore on, I *knew* this wasn't a good idea.

After class Dr. Briggs took me aside and said gently, "You organized this debate very well. But you know, I don't think you've ever had such a diverse class before. It presents new challenges."

I thought about the students: Korean, Chinese, Japanese, European, Hispanic, Romanian, and Indian. All put together in one classroom. In *my* classroom.

"With so many ethnic and cultural backgrounds," Dr. Briggs continued, "a debate will almost never work." He paused. "Get the students to work together as much as possible. Have them help each other."

The next week papers were due that got graded by the entire English Department faculty. And so I tried another new idea: I had the students help each other with their papers—read them to each other, give each other pointers on writing clearly and skillfully.

And it worked! As a class their papers received much higher grades than they had had the past grading session.

I guess that's what I mean by learning from teaching. I learned that diversity is great. That is, when we use our diverse viewpoints not to argue with each other, but to help each other.

"We who are strong ought to bear with the failings of the weak and not to please ourselves. Each of us should please his neighbor for his good, to build him up" (Romans 15:1, 2).

Lori

Spills and Thrills

On Father's Day in 1995, 34-year-old Steven Trotter and his friend, Lori Martin, climbed into a Fiberglass-and-Kevlar-covered steel barrel. Steven's brother and a couple of friends floated the barrel down the Niagara River and then watched it plunge over 180-foot-high Niagara Falls.

Steven and Lori were strapped inside. They wore knee and elbow pads and helmets and life preservers. And they breathed from air tanks fitted inside the 6' x 10' barrel, which took six years and $25,000 to build. They survived with bumps and bruises.

Emergency rescue workers who recovered the barrel had to descend a slippery 150-foot cliff by rope into what one of them described as a cross between a hurricane and a tornado. They found the barrel swirling in an eddy near the base of the falls, close to a tourist attraction called Scenic Tunnels. The workers arrested Steven and Lori, then took them to a hospital.

Steven had dropped over the falls in a barrel before. His 1985 trip left him with a fractured disk in his back. Now he and his friend have set a record as the only male-female team to survive the plunge. They represented the fifteenth successful attempt to ride the Falls. Four people have died trying to make the plunge this century.

Why would anyone do this? For the same reason one might go skydiving, bungee-jumping, or swinging from the Golden Gate Bridge, all of which Steven Trotter has done. His sister Cindy said, "He loves the thrill of it."

You may start down that road too, looking for the next big thrill, and you'll discover that "the eye never has enough of seeing, nor the ear its fill of hearing" (Ecclesiastes 1:8). The last thrill is never enough.

God gave us the capacity to be thrilled. He put adrenaline in our bodies. When we commit ourselves to God, we turn all our capacities over to Him. Even the desire for an adrenaline rush goes to Him. Everything we are, we place in service for Him. "Fear God and keep his commandments, for this is the whole duty of man" (Ecclesiastes 12:13).

By the way, the last I heard, Steven Trotter was facing a $25,000 fine. Big thrill.

"I wanted to see what was worthwhile for men to do under heaven during the few days of their lives. . . . I denied myself nothing my eyes desired; I refused my heart no pleasure. . . . Yet when I surveyed all that my hands had done and what I had toiled to achieve, everything was meaningless, a chasing after the wind" (Ecclesiastes 2:3-11).

Tim

Say What?

Here's a little quiz for you. Just one thing—you can't use a dictionary. Now, see if you can guess the real meaning of the words below. Circle the answer you think is correct.

gesneriad
   a. a legendary creature that is half serpent and half human

b. an Egyptian bromeliad

c. the byproduct of gestation in arachnids

d. a family of tropical herbs such as an African violet

e. an algebraic term designating the point at which concentric circles overlap to the point of infinity

juba

a. a dance of Southern plantation Blacks

b. a musical instrument of Saratonga that produces a series of notes by blowing across cut reeds

c. a form of Hungarian dance

d. a generic greeting used in the conversation of Somalian people

e. a high-pitched reed instrument used in the West Indies

ultimogeniture

a. the process by which an Englishman becomes a "gentleman's gentleman"

b. the highest ranking at the sperm bank

c. a system of inheritance by which the youngest child succeeds to the estate

d. the armature unit of an X-ray machine

e. a gene occupying the twenty-third position on the X chromosome that is chiefly responsible for skeleton structure

eriophyid

a. the area in which two or more concentric circles overlap

b. any of a large family of minute plant-feeding mites that have two pairs of legs

c. the third stage of plant mitosis

d. an underwater sea urchin found only in the South Pacific

e. a gland located above the urethra that functions as a screening device and properly routes bodily waste

The answers are at the end of this reading. How'd you do? Did we fool you?

Yesterday during youth group we played "Fictionary." Each person picked an uncommon word out of the dictionary and wrote the correct definition on a piece of paper. Then everyone else made up fake definitions. (That's where this quiz came from.)

Then we had to do what you just did—try to guess the real definition as someone read them off for us. And every single time, with every single word, someone faked someone else out! Sometimes almost all of us were fooled. We were all pretty good at deceiving one another.

Now, that's not something to be proud of. Because that goes against God's way of doing things. God is upfront, honest, and always trustworthy.

We talked about that, too. How easy it is to lie to people, and how wrong.

We decided we want to be trustworthy. We want to be like God. And that means carefully guarding our words and our actions, leaving behind lies and hypocrisy for truth and transparency.

Answers: d, a, c, b

"The Lord detests lying lips, but he delights in men who are truthful" (Proverbs 12:22).

Lori

Rock 'n' Roll

Cruising along a wet mountain road, I saw a rock up ahead in the middle of the asphalt. With just a couple of seconds to decide what to do, I went with the thought that it looked pretty small and drove straight over it.

As my Honda Civic bounced into the air, a series of huge, booming sounds under the car said to me, "Stupid move." I felt the ripple from front to back as the rock rolled underneath and out behind me.

Pulling over to the side of the road, I began to think up various stories to offer my wife, who was following several minutes behind in our other car. I looked underneath the Civic.

The rock had indented a corner shape at the bottom of the front spoiler, passed between the left steering rod and the side of the engine, pushed up the floor—front and back—on the driver's side, left a muddy scratch on the rear axle and a dent in the fuel tank, and pulled a corner shape out of the rear trim.

But was it just luck that my car had ground up a boulder and come down without serious damage? Was it a coincidence that I did not bust a steering rod 150 miles from home on an isolated road?

My quick answer is that all good things come from God, so it wasn't luck. Not that you can find a pattern or a cause-and-effect link from these events. But I know that everything that makes my life happier comes from Him.

Sure, God doesn't stand in the way of trials sometimes. He told us through James to "consider it pure joy . . . whenever you face trials of many kinds, because . . . the testing of your faith develops perseverance" (James 1:2). So "those who suffer according to God's will should commit themselves to their faithful Creator and continue to do good" (1 Peter 4:19).

But I thank the Lord for the help I seem to get now and then. I don't ask Him to smooth everything out for me, because that would make me grotesquely selfish. But I praise God that He spoils us now and then, knowing that He's not hurting our progress toward heaven.

"Who of you by worrying can add a single hour to his life? Since you cannot do this very little thing, why do you worry about the rest?" (Luke 12:25, 26).

Tim

Age to Age

The first apartment complex I lived in was old. Water ran rusty through the faucets. And every resident's balcony was decorated with bright patio furniture and flower boxes.

Seventy percent of the people who lived at Willow Tree Circle apartments were on Social Security.

The night I moved in they were all sitting on their balconies. I think they postponed their bedtimes to watch us carry the last load—my stereo speakers—up to the top floor. I just knew what they were thinking.

Here comes someone young. Why does she want to live here? They've taken over the world; now they have to invade our apartment complex. Well, here goes our peaceful retirement. Now we'll have to listen to wild parties and rock music. Look at the size of those speakers.

I knew they wouldn't want me in their building. And I wasn't sure I was going to like it either. I'd have to watch what kind of music I played and how noisy I was after 8:00 p.m., when I was sure they all went to bed.

But here we were, drawn together by our preference for sunny sitting rooms, built-in bookshelves, balconies and oak floors, green lawns and willow trees. Here we were living together.

The first month I learned that I had to shuffle through four issues of *Modern Maturity* beneath the mailboxes to get to my *Glamour* magazine. And the bookmobile blocked the driveway on Tuesday afternoons.

Then I found out why benches lined the sidewalk along the buildings. It was so Doris, on her morning walk, could sit and rest when she got tired. And so the Osbornes could catch their breath before climbing the stairs to their second-floor apartment.

One week an ambulance pulled up in front of the building. The Cramers across the hall told me that paramedics were taking Mrs. Daily to the hospital. She'd had another stroke.

85

But I was surprised at Willow Tree Circle. You could usually hear Florence Richmond's TV from the hall. Sometimes I had to drown it out with my stereo. And the Emericks, who never closed their drapes, always watched the 11:00 p.m. news. Before I got my TV, I could sit on my balcony and watch theirs.

I also learned at Willow Creek Circle.

At least every other day the lock on my mailbox stuck and wouldn't open. One day when I got home from work I put the key in the mail slot, but it wouldn't turn. Then the key wouldn't even come back out.

I began to tug on it in frustration. The row of mailboxes banged loudly, and I felt better. Suddenly three apartment doors opened, and the residents stared out at me.

Don't worry; I'm not stealing your retirement checks, I grumbled silently.

The next day the mailbox wouldn't work again. *This is too much,* I thought. *I will not be outdone by a mailbox.*

I tugged on the key. Mr. Cramer was getting his mail.

"Here, let me help you," he offered.

Reluctantly I wrenched the key out of the slot and handed it to him.

He turned it over in his hands and studied it a moment. Then he positioned it in front of the slot and slowly slid it in.

"These things can be temperamental," he said, as if talking about a horse. He bent over and put his eyes to the mailbox, then turned the key, as carefully as if he were opening a safe.

Well, I could have done this, I thought impatiently.

And then the mailbox opened, and I thanked him, realizing that no, I couldn't have done this. Or I *wouldn't* have done this. I didn't have Mr. Cramer's patience, something I could learn from him.

Another day I went to the laundry room. Since laundry was 75 cents a load, I stuffed as much of it into a washer as I could fit.

I started the cycle and went back upstairs to clean my apartment. When I returned, a white-haired man was standing beside my washer. "Is that your wash in there?" he asked nervously.

"Yes."

"It was jumping around so much I thought the machine was going to come out of the wall. I stopped it and rearranged the clothes.

Sometimes it gets off balance. I hope that was all right—"

"No, I mean, yes. Thank you," I said, surprised.

"Mine does that too sometimes," he began. "I usually stay down here to watch it."

I don't have time to watch my laundry change cycles, I thought as he transferred his clothes from a washer to a dryer. I noticed he had only shirts and pants, no dresses or female things.

"I've lived here only two months." He took two quarters out of his pocket. "My wife just died." He fiddled with the coin slot. The quarters fell to the floor. Slowly he bent to pick them up.

"Let me help you," I said.

"These coin slots are so thin. I can't always see them."

I slid the quarters in for him, and he patted my shoulder. "You're young," he smiled wistfully.

The residents of Willow Creek Circle liked me because I was young. Because I got dressed up and went to work every morning. Because to them I moved quickly, backed out of my parking space frighteningly fast, and had an exciting life. I went places. I had friends over.

I liked them because they were old. Because they knew everything about our town. (They liked to tell me about the coldest winter "back in '36.") Because to me their lives were peaceful, settled, comfortable, content. Because they were home when I needed them, and they had time to listen and history to tell me.

Don't let anyone tell you there's no generation gap. There is, and it's one of the nicest things in life.

We lived together in Willow Tree Circle. And we lived well.

"Is not wisdom found among the aged? Does not long life bring understanding?" (Job 12:12).

Lori

Get Into Heaven

A m I going to be in heaven?" That's the big question several teens put down on an *Insight* survey. A few others mentioned the question "Am I witnessing to my non-Christian friends?"

I think these two questions amount to the same thing. If you have turned your life over to Jesus, you *will* be in heaven. And if you've turned your life over to Jesus, you won't be able to stop yourself from witnessing, in one way or another, about your faith.

These questions tell me a lot. They tell me that many of you are thinking about where we're going—heaven. You have your eye on the goal, not just on your cornflakes in the morning. And you want your friends to be in heaven too.

I also see that you aren't completely sure of your place in heaven. Will you waver, fall off the path, and rebel before the end comes?

The only barrier to reaching heaven is your sin, and you know that Jesus has taken that monster out. So let me offer a couple of sentences that will work for you at any moment in the future:

You may fall into some sin every day, but if you turn back to God the same day and ask forgiveness, then your place in heaven is absolutely sure.

If you let the sins pile up or let your attitude turn sour and selfish, and then you catch yourself, go to God and say you're sorry. Then drop it, just like He does. Your place is sure.

If someone else catches you in a sin and pulls you up short, you may be angry for a while. When you get over it, go to God, say you're sorry, and drop it. Knowing that Jesus' sacrifice will clean you up if you submit to Him, you will know your place is sure.

If you think you've failed as a witness because of a sin, go to God for forgiveness and get cleaned up inside. Then ask Him to use your actions for good somehow. He's got more power to do that than you can begin to imagine. And His power bursts into action when you pray specifically for friends and fellow students and anyone else you meet.

I've just given you a working definition for repentance without using the word. Works every time. Use it, and go to heaven!

"This calls for patient endurance on the part of the saints who obey God's commandments and remain faithful to Jesus" *(Revelation 14:12).*

Tim

Taking the Plunge

49

S *plash!*
Gag, swallow, cough.

"I don't think I like this," I croaked to Kim, who was trying to teach me how to snorkel.

"Try again," he coaxed.

Splash!

Gag, swallow, cough.

"I can't breathe," I sputtered, ripping off my headgear and spitting saltwater.

"Your snorkel's full of water. You have to clear it," said my enthusiastic husband.

We were newlyweds vacationing in St. Croix, and Kim was just dying to show me the view below the aqua ocean.

"I have an idea!" He jumped out of the water, pulling me behind him.

Soon we were both standing in the shower in our bathing suits. I tightened the snorkel and mask around my head. Kim poured a cupful of tap water into the snorkel and yelled, "OK, blow it out!"

Spurt. Splash!

"Good," he praised. "Right in my face." He filled the snorkel again. And again. And again.

Soon I had the hang of clearing it and breathing through it, so we ran back outside and into the sea.

I'll never forget that first plunge below the surface. Suddenly I was in a quiet, slow-moving world of Crayola-colored fish: yellow and midnight-blue and aqua and orange and red. They were beautiful!

It was quiet, too. I could hear only the low munch, munch of parrot fish chewing on coral.

Just a few weeks ago Kim and I took another vacation underwater.

"Wow, it's a whole different world down here," I said as we stuck our faces into the warm Caribbean. "I've missed it."

We followed parrot fish through rock formations, fed hungry yellowtail snappers, and spied camouflaged sand divers.

We decided that God sure has a great sense of sight and touch and smell and taste. Everything beautiful and restful comes from Him.

On Sabbath afternoon we plunged under the sea again. And it was a spiritual day with Him and His creation.

"Great are the works of the Lord; they are pondered by all who delight in them" (Psalm 111:2).

Lori

Jesus Is Still the Answer

Kurt Cobain lived an unhappy life.

His parents divorced when he was 8. Punted from one set of relatives to another, he didn't know who really cared about him. So it isn't surprising that the music he wrote for Nirvana spoke mostly about two things: pain and alienation.

It's also not surprising that he felt constant physical pain from an ailment called irritable bowel syndrome. With a background like that, I would have had a physical reaction too. The pain he endured every day drove him to think he didn't want to live anymore. And the drugs he took to escape life just made it worse.

After Cobain's suicide, lots of his fans called hot lines and radio stations. They felt grief and wanted to understand. Some of them were angry that he took a cheap and easy way out.

I felt depressed myself when I read about what he did. I realized that he was a person without hope.

It may seem strange to say that knowing Jesus would have been the answer to Kurt Cobain's problems. But think about this. Didn't Kurt need to know that life has a purpose? Didn't he need to feel unconditional love? Didn't he need to glimpse an alternative existence besides the darkness of his pain and loneliness?

I think he did need to know those things. Jesus lifts you up above the pain, because He provides all the things you need. I wish Kurt hadn't missed out on that.

Perhaps Kurt thought about God. Maybe he thought God seemed too distant. Maybe he blamed God for all the tragedy and pain dumped on him. But the truth is that only the devil could have dumped those things on him.

Getting to know and trust God is like flipping the switch of a huge light. The love He has for us becomes visible. The great things He wants for our future show up, including living into forever with endless things to do and no problems, guaranteed.

Once that light goes on, we see that God has provided not an escape, but a solution.

"Oh, the joys of those who do not follow the advice of the wicked, or stand around with sinners. . . . They delight in doing everything the Lord wants. . . . Their leaves never wither, and in all they do, they prosper" (Psalm 1:1-3, NLT).

Tim

Ouch

I don't do very well around glass. I think I'm too rough or clumsy. Take our wedding gifts. Crystal bowls. Water goblets. Glass candlesticks. All just a memory.

My husband noticed the other day that we have three pieces of stemware left from our 12-piece set. And only one breakable wedding gift has survived in our home—a small cut-glass candy dish.

A few weeks ago I broke a drinking glass. It shattered all over the kitchen floor. So I swept up the mess, but I must have missed a spot.

The next morning, walking barefoot, I found a shard of glass. Actually, the bottom of my foot found it.

After saying "Ouch," I hopped on the other foot to the couch. I had my husband look. Neither of us could see anything but a little blood.

He got a flashlight and shone it on the foot. We poured hydrogen peroxide over the wound. We still saw nothing, but when I pressed the spot it hurt bad.

Finally we got an operating instrument: a straight pin from my sewing kit. After careful sterilization (with a match), we began to pick apart the tough skin on the bottom of my foot.

At first it really looked like we were causing more damage. We were tearing up skin that looked perfectly fine. But when we finally got deep enough and saw a shiny sliver of glass, we nodded. That was the culprit.

That tiny piece of glass stuck beneath the skin had hardly made a mark going in, but every time I had moved or tried to walk, it had kept cutting the flesh beneath the surface. It hurt to remove it, but as soon as it was gone . . . total relief. I could press on my foot and walk without pain.

That piece of glass reminds me of sin. Cherished sin I sometimes keep just beneath the surface, not obvious to most people. But very damaging.

Sin, like shards of glass, tears up our insides. Maybe we see only a trickle of blood from time to time, but inside the healthy skin is becoming torn and infected.

What we need to do is have our Physician remove it. It might hurt as He tears through those layers. But once it's gone we'll love the relief.

"God disciplines us for our good, that we may share in his holiness. No discipline seems pleasant at the time, but painful. Later on, however, it produces a harvest of righteousness and peace for those who have been trained by it" (Hebrews 12:10, 11). —Lori

I Said "Jesus"

Do you feel funny when you say the word "Jesus"? It seems weird, but lots of Adventists, young and old, feel awkward saying "Jesus." And inhibition keeps them from talking about what He's done for them.

I didn't notice this phenomenon until I read an article in *Signs of the Times*. A writer in her 30s observed that she's part of a generation that never actually refers to Jesus by His name in conversation. It's something her generation avoids out of fear or shyness or who knows what. The phenomenon afflicts other generations, too.

This is very strange when you realize that Jesus is what we're about. Without Him, we have nothing; we would be up a creek with a time bomb. He's the reason we're not the walking dead.

Perhaps we feel awkward about the name of Jesus because we sang His name in little kiddie songs. If you went to junior Sabbath school, you might have picked up the idea that Jesus counts for children and babies. For grown-ups, there's hard reality.

But this is a fatal misconception. And I mean *fatal*.

Talking about our experience with Jesus may make us feel as though we're boasting about our superior piety. More likely we feel as though we're inflating the status of a neglected relationship.

I don't know about you, but if I air the details of my life with Jesus, I feel pressure to stick to the truth. Often I'd prefer to keep the truth to myself. So it's easier just to avoid the whole subject.

One of the regrets that stays with me is that I never pushed my parents to explain to me their particular way of relating to Jesus. They had a few more years of practice than I did, and their insights would surely have clued me in to Jesus' priceless value. It took me years more to find out on my own.

So go bug your parents or your pastor. Ask them, "What does Jesus mean to you? How do you relate to Him? What's He done for you?" You may not want to copy what they do, but you'll know what they've found.

"Therefore, holy brothers, who share in the heavenly calling, fix your thoughts on Jesus, the apostle and high priest whom we confess" (Hebrews 3:1).

Tim

Behind the Scenes

Last weekend Kim and I visited some relatives who own a hotel. They let us act as though *we* owned the place. We swam in the pool, lay on the beach chairs, and rode the elevator to the top (locked) floor. We even got free hot fudge sundaes from the soda shop.

Then Sunday morning an emergency came up. An employee hadn't shown up for work. Someone who worked in the hotel laundry. The other employees couldn't turn dirty sheets and towels into clean ones fast enough for the attendants cleaning the rooms.

So our host changed out of her suit to do laundry herself.

Kim and I looked at each other. "We'll help," we said.

She fussed and objected, but finally saw our determination. We actually thought it might be fun.

And it was.

She led us into a hot, steamy room and introduced us to Norma. Norma showed us how to feed long, wet sheets into a machine that dries and irons and half folds them all in one run.

So we fed it and watched sheet after sheet, pillowcase after pillowcase, go through, and I thought about the people on vacation who would sleep on those clean sheets tonight. And about how many times I've taken clean sheets for granted. And about how fun sometimes it is to get a behind-the-scenes look.

Then I remembered a sermon I'd heard my dad give. He'd talked about Jesus' miracles. And he'd pointed out that the servants were the people who got to see the most miracles.

Take the wedding feast at Cana. Jesus' mother brought Him into the kitchen and told Him that the servants had run out of wine.

Jesus saw six stone water jars sitting nearby, and He said to the servants, "Fill the jars with water." They did, and then He told them to draw some out and give it to their master.

Again they did what He said, and their master praised it. John 2:9 says that the master did not realize where it had come from, though the servants who had drawn the water knew.

Only those behind the scenes saw the miracle. Not the host. Not the partyers. But the *servants*. They even had a part in the miracle.

Think about the feeding of the 5,000. If you had been one in the crowd, maybe you wouldn't have known where the food came from. But if you had been the person who had donated your small lunch, or a disciple who had helped pass it out, you would have been a firsthand witness and a participant in the wonder.

Sometimes the best place to be is not out on the beach or on stage, but in the laundry or kitchen. Places where people serve. Places where miracles happen.

"Jesus said to the servants, 'Fill the jars with water'; so they filled them to the brim. Then he told them, 'Now draw some out and take it to the master of the banquet.' They did so, and the master of the banquet tasted the water that had been turned into wine. He did not realize where it had come from, though the servants who had drawn the water knew" (John 2:7-9).

Lori

54
People Still Getting AIDS

You never forget your first encounter with someone who has AIDS. Ask Paul Fournier, a teenage Canadian who went on the first *Insight* Extreme Workout mission trip to San Francisco.

All day Paul handed out free food to people who were HIV-positive but who looked fairly healthy. And then he met a man with lesions all over his face.

A report released by the White House in March 1996 showed that about 25 percent of Americans who become infected with HIV each year are under age 20. Teenagers, in other words.

Why does it happen? It's not because they are ignorant of the disease or the dangers. It happens because they choose to engage in high-risk behavior anyway.

If you are straight and plan to remain a virgin or celibate, you may think this comes nowhere near you. But these life-and-death issues have a way of affecting all of us sooner or later. I personally know someone I went to college with who died of AIDS because of one risky sexual encounter.

Someone you know may make the same mistake. Don't let it happen to them or you.

The basic truth remains in effect. God designed male and female for each other in a marriage situation. Fooling around with any of the other alternatives may feel good at a certain point, but it will wreck your life, and it may kill you.

Paul Fournier handed the bag of food to that man with AIDS and shook his hand. The man is certainly dead now.

"Come to me, all you who are weary and burdened, and I will give you rest. . . . My yoke is easy and my burden is light" (Matthew 11:28-30).

Tim

One Saturday Night

Bill and Pat welcomed us with hugs and Florida smiles. (They used to live there, and still radiate the warmth during Maryland winters.) They're the kind of friends who swing the doors wide every Saturday night for group fun.

It goes like this: you bring sandwich fixings—whatever's in your refrigerator and cupboard—and fruit to add to Pat's famous tub of fruit salad. (She always adds bags of blueberries she and her husband picked and froze last summer.)

When Kim and I arrived at 6:20, the group was already singing. Dave played the piano, and Pat and Bill were making sure the new dentist and his wife and daughters, and the kids who'd come up from the academy, knew all the songs.

After singing, Bill pulled out a grocery bag and explained

tonight's worship activity. Everyone would reach in and pull something out (he'd gathered miscellaneous objects from around the house, yard, and garage). We'd go around the circle, each telling what Bible story our object reminded us of or what spiritual lesson we could draw from it.

Robbie, the academy freshman who got red cinnamon-flavored dental floss, exclaimed, "Yeah! I'm brimming with ideas!" But he did manage to think of Rahab tossing the scarlet cord down to Joshua's spies.

"A scarlet cord of dental floss? Hmmm . . . We never thought of that before," came responses.

There were references to Jesus as the light of the world by those who got a light bulb or a flashlight. Jesus as the Rock of Ages from the boy who lifted out a rock. And the observation (from the person who got a roll of film) about how we tend to leave an unfinished roll of film in our camera for months, but as soon as we've used it up, we want it developed in an hour—at the most. We can't wait to see the pictures.

"If only we had that kind of excited anticipation about heaven," this person said. "We'd get a lot more people excited about it."

After we'd all finished drawing a lesson and dropped our objects back into the bag, Bill turned to Dave, still sitting on the piano bench. "Ready to tell us your story now, Dave?" Bill asked.

"Sure." Dave nodded and sat up. He began to tell us about his 20-year high school reunion coming in April. "Wendy and I went to meet with the planning committee this week," he said. "The first challenge is to locate and contact all our old classmates."

He looked around. "I don't know if we had a worse class than most, or if all classes are this way. But those of us on the planning committee were comparing information about where everybody is now. We've had several classmates in jail, many who don't attend church and aren't in contact with anybody anymore, and then, of course, some who are very successful, and some very active in church work."

The room was quiet.

"As I listened to the update on some old classmates and friends, buddies I'd hung around with, I wondered if we could have done more for them." Dave paused. "You know, if we could have encouraged them more in their Christian struggle. Maybe asked a friend, 'How are you doing spiritually?' or 'How's your friendship with Jesus?'

"Could we have even been better *listeners?*" Dave continued. "Does the Holy Spirit not only help us talk to friends about Jesus, but listen to them as well, and encourage them to talk about Him?"

Most of Dave's listeners were looking down now, some probably calling back faces of school friends they might have touched, some thinking of classmates right there in the room with them.

"I don't mean to depress us," Dave said, smiling apologetically, "but I just wanted to share these thoughts. Maybe we can do more for the people we hang around with. Maybe even change how their lives will turn out. I don't know. It's just something to think about for some of you academy students, and us older folks, too. We all still have the future."

There was a pause then, some nods, and quiet amens before Bill prayed. And then the women went to the kitchen to make egg salad and vegetarian Reuben sandwiches.

And to the sound of the popcorn kernels exploding and the men setting up the Pictionary game, we all thought a little more seriously about what influence we might be having on our friends. How we might, just in our conversations and attitudes about God, be leading a friend away from Him or encouraging a friend toward Him.

I remembered my group of friends in academy and thought of where they each are now. No, I probably didn't change them a lot for eternity.

But I have the future. So do you.

"See to it, brothers, that none of you has a sinful, unbelieving heart that turns away from the living God. But encourage one another daily, as long as it is called Today, so that none of you may be hardened by sin's deceitfulness" (Hebrews 3:12, 13). *Lori*

Rolling a Stone up a Mountain

C heck this quote. "It is not that Christianity has been tried and found wanting. It has been found difficult and not tried" (attributed to G. K. Chesterton by William Plache in "Why Bother With Theology?" *Christian Century*, Feb. 2-9, 1994).

Is it really difficult to be a Christian? God promises love and acceptance and peace of mind and eternal life. I don't find a lot of difficulty to face in that list. But I don't think being a Christian is easy.

In order to receive these gifts from God, we have to be willing to accept them and experience them, which means going against just about everyone around us and many things inside us.

The difficulty starts with the fact that even though we might want to do the right thing, we still want to answer to ourselves only. Who is going to decide what I do or do not do? *I am.* We really do not want God to be looking over our shoulders *every* minute. Kind of cramps our style, doesn't it?

Truth is, though, life is difficult whether you control your life or God does. You already know from looking at the world around you (you do that, right?) that people have come up with infinite ways to cause themselves difficulties. And some of them believe that they can avoid God *and* avoid difficulty if they are just careful or wealthy or educated or tough enough. But that is a myth.

Following God (Christianity) is difficult because you have to let go of every area of your life, even the pet ones you want to manage yourself, and let God take over. This is a hugely radical step. Think about it long and hard before you go for it. Doing it by halves won't work.

So if you think following God is difficult because He seems to be saying "Don't do this, don't do that," remember this:

"Contrary to popular opinion, sin is not what you want to do but can't; it is what you should not do because it will hurt you—and hurt you bad. . . .

"God is not a policeman; He is a Father concerned about His children. When a child picks up a snake and the father says, 'Put that down right this minute!' the child thinks he is losing a toy. The fact is, he is not losing a toy; he is losing a snake" (Steve Brown, in *Key Life,* July-August 1994, quoted in *Christianity Today,* Oct. 3, 1994, p. 61).

Letting go of the snake is difficult sometimes, but it will ultimately make you happy and save your life.

"If you live according to the sinful nature, you will die; but if by the Spirit you put to death the misdeeds of the body, you will live" *(Romans 8:13).*

Tim

57
Get Up

"Home again!" I said to myself as the plane landed.

I grabbed my carry-on bag and headed to the shuttle that would take us to the airport terminal. I snatched the first seat I came to, one by the doors. Passengers filed in after me until we were packed tight—wall-to-wall people and bags, standing room only.

Just when I thought no one else could fit, a young couple entered. They looked out of breath. The woman carried a small baby wrapped in a blanket. Her husband, loaded down with a diaper bag and a folded stroller, looked around for a place they could stand.

The shuttle engine started, and the woman leaned against a pole for support, cradling the sleeping baby in both arms. Her husband tried to hold on to her and the baby, glancing around nervously.

"I'm OK," she whispered, smiling with large dark eyes.

"No," he said, shaking his head. Again he looked around for a protected place for his family.

They stood right beside me. I was a little slow, but suddenly I realized the solution. "Would you like to sit here?" I asked her.

"No, no, I'm fine," she said, smiling again and rocking her baby.

The shuttle began to move. The husband looked worried and tried to steady his wife.

"Here, you can sit here," I said again, this time standing up and offering her my seat.

"Thank you," she said, sinking down on the vinyl. The baby began to coo.

"Thank you," her husband said, relaxing.

When we stopped at the terminal, the pretty dark-haired woman smiled at me. "Thank you for giving up your seat. That was so thoughtful."

"Yes, thank you," her husband repeated, nodding.

"No problem," I said. And I meant it. It had been nothing.

But it got me thinking. When doing the kind thing is so simple, easy, and rewarding, why don't I do it more often?

And why are people hesitant to accept good deeds? Do they know when we don't really mean it? After all, offering to give up my seat didn't work. I actually had to get up and give it up.

So maybe instead of saying "I wish I could help Scott pass algebra," I need to go to Scott's house and help him study to pass his class. Maybe I have to stop saying "Give me a call if there's anything I can do" and *do something*.

I wasn't around to give my bed in Bethlehem to Baby Jesus and His parents. But the amazing thing is that when I give my seat to a baby boy and his mother, I'm kind of doing it for Jesus after all.

"Each of you should look not only to your own interests, but also to the interests of others. Your attitude should be the same as that of Christ Jesus: who, being in very nature God, did not consider equality with God something to be grasped, but made himself nothing, taking the very nature of a servant" (Philippians 2:4-7).

Lori

Are We Having Any Fun Yet?

I read this book you would love, called *Millennial Fever and the End of the World*. OK, don't go snoozing on me. It's about the preachers who got millions of people riled up about the second coming of Jesus in the early 1800s.

But that was more than 150 years ago, right? What's the deal?

For 10 years they preached that Jesus was coming any day now, and you'd better get ready or you're gonna burn. Lots of people laughed at them, and even lots of other preachers cut them down. People scorned them by calling them "Adventists." This was before any Adventist church formed.

Maybe you know that those "Adventists" back then, especially William Miller, had it right about one event (the judgment) and wrong about another (the Second Coming). They thought that the verse which says no one knows the day or the hour of the coming of the Son of man meant that you couldn't fix the exact day. But that didn't mean you couldn't fix the year or perhaps the month.

You know what went down. In 1844 the "Adventists" gave everything away. They didn't plant crops for food. They had no money or clothes left. And on October 22 those believers waited up all night and *nothing happened*.

How much faith would you have after that kind of embarrassment? Would you preach the Second Coming after you had to go to Snidely Whiplash next door and ask for some food to cover you until spring?

Well, some people kept preaching it. And they still are. Seventh-day Adventists believe that the day those early Adventists were looking for *will* come. We have faith that Jesus wasn't talking empty promises. The fact that we don't know which day it will be makes no difference. He's coming back.

"The Lord himself will come down from heaven, with a loud command, with the voice of the archangel and with the trumpet call of God, and the dead in Christ will rise first. After that, we who are still alive and are left will be caught up together with them in the clouds to meet the Lord in the air. And so we will be with the Lord forever" (1 Thessalonians 4:16, 17).

Tim

You Oughta Be in Pictures

Around Mother's Day last year I went looking through my photo albums for pictures of my mom. I expected to find bunches of them: Mom holding me as a baby, Mom and me under the Christmas tree, at the beach, at my birthday parties, at my eighth-grade graduation.

But I was disappointed. Because I couldn't find pictures of Mom and me together. Just my sister and me. My dad and sister and me. My grandpa and grandma and cousins and me. Grade-school friends and boyfriends and me.

Where was Mom hiding?

Then I realized. Mom was behind the camera!

Through my entire growing up, Mom was busy recording the moments, treasuring the memories, making events special for me.

On the edge of lots of pictures I can even see Mom's finger. (She had a tendency to slide it over the lens.) Yup, she was there all right. There smiling at me and blinding me with flashes of importance.

That's why I was interested in reading about Jesus' mother, Mary. Luke records the awesome events around Jesus' birth and childhood. Then he says, "Mary treasured up all these things and pondered them in her heart."

That's what moms do. They remember. When we had chicken pox. How we got that scar on our finger. What we said to Jesus the first time we prayed.

Maybe they don't get in many pictures, but that doesn't mean they weren't there or shouldn't be remembered.

Here's an idea: Take a picture with your mom. Just you and her. And keep it around. It's time to give her your spotlight.

"Honor your father and your mother, as the Lord your God has commanded you, so that you may live long and that it may go well with you" (Deuteronomy 5:16).

Fuel for Thought

I stopped at a gas station while rushing to the airport to meet my father-in-law. At the first pump, I filled the tank to the top. Then I noticed the sign on the pump. "DIESEL."

Now, diesel fuel has less than half the power of regular gas. So fill up your car with diesel, and watch it sputter like a sick lawn mower and die. Praise the Lord, I did not start up my car.

In about 15 seconds I realized that I needed a tow truck, a mechanic, a taxicab, and a rental car. And I had about 10 minutes to find them.

I think about God in every situation, good or bad. And I began to wonder, *Is this one of those learning things, Lord?*

I slouched inside and announced to the two gas station employees that I had filled my car with diesel and needed a tow truck. One of them, Dwayne, called for the tow truck owned by the gas station. Then he called a cab. I wish every Christian I have ever met were as friendly and helpful as Dwayne.

Thinking I would have to wait 10 minutes, I walked to the restroom. I hadn't been in there five seconds when Dwayne yelled through the door, "The cab's here!" I began to think that this catastrophe was being resolved far too easily.

The cabby, a man from Ghana, asked about my troubles. As we drove I gave him my excuse for filling up with diesel: Our 2-week-old baby was keeping Linda and me awake at night, and I was dead tired.

The cab ride cost $7.20, but I had only $5. He took the five and told me not to worry. Another saint. My father-in-law had been waiting only five minutes when I met him. We picked up a rental car at the Alamo Express counter. No problem.

The next morning I drove to the auto repair shop and watched as 14 gallons of diesel poured out into a drum. Total amount I paid to various helpful individuals along the way: $190.

Did God cause this to happen? I think not. Did He allow it to happen? Yes. Did I learn a lesson? I learned a few small ones, but I really don't know why such things happen. I am content to wait for an explanation, because God always gives answers in His time. And the peace of mind I felt through this episode was a gift from Him.

By the way, I met the same cab driver at the same gas station the next day. He's never been more surprised in his life to get a late payment and a tip. Tell me God didn't plan that one.

"The wise man has eyes in his head, while the fool walks in the darkness; but I came to realize that the same fate overtakes them both" (Ecclesiastes 2:14).

Tim

My Favorite Place

I think I've found my favorite place on earth.

Last January Kim and I met our families on the island of Maui. We gave up Christmas presents and saved our money to go there instead.

It was worth it. We spent seven days snorkeling in fish-rich water, eating macadamia everything, and learning how to surf (I got up!).

Now, to my favorite spot. One evening we took this paved walk behind the hotels in Wailea. The walk goes along the ocean, so as you stroll you can watch the sunset.

I still remember the orange ball sinking below the palm trees while the waves glimmered. And as the evening grew darker, luau music and tiki torches brightened the balmy night along the waterfront. I didn't think I could ever be happier.

My dad, a pastor, was invited to preach that Sabbath. He told the members of the Maui Seventh-day Adventist Church, "After spending a week here, I don't know how you motivate people to want to go to heaven!"

I felt the same way. When you're in paradise, why do you need heaven?

But the people in Hawaii said they long for heaven, and they seemed to mean it. That Sabbath a large group at church told us they'd come to the island for the funeral of their young cousin who had died of cancer. One teen was hurting because she'd given up a non-Christian boyfriend to follow God.

Even people on beautiful islands want to go to God's kingdom. Because no place on earth is safe from Satan's and sin's effects. Only Jesus knows the way to Paradise.

"No eye has seen, no ear has heard, no mind has conceived what God has prepared for those who love him" (1 Corinthians 2:9).

Lori

The Ten Do's

If you think the Ten Commandments keep telling you, "Don't do this, don't do that," maybe you've never noticed what they ask you to do.

1. Put God before everything and everyone else in your life.
2. Worship God instead of things.
3. Use God's name in reverence.
4. Keep the Sabbath day holy, and rest on it.
5. Respect all of your parents.
6. Respect and protect the life of others.
7. Remain faithful to your friends, your boyfriend/girlfriend, your spouse, and remain pure.
8. Respect the property of others.
9. Tell the truth always.
10. Be content with what you have at any given moment.

You may have some of these up and running in your life (most people in the world think number 6 is a must) and some of them maybe not yet. But don't worry. You really only need to worry about number 1.

What you may have found, as I have, is that if you try really, really hard to do numbers 2-10 but don't do number 1, you end up failing big-time. But if you do number 1, you'll no longer be holding God at arm's length, and then you'll allow Him to help you do 2, 3, 4, 5, 6, 7, 8, 9, and 10. In fact, He does all the work at that point because you and I cannot.

Remember, the Ten Do's make no sense if you don't know God. If they bother you, find out a little more about who God really is. Hint: There's a reason some people are saying so many glowing, positive things about God. These facts may seem like well-kept secrets in our church, but they're true.

"If anyone loves me, he will obey my teaching. My Father will love him, and we will come to him and make our home with him" *(John 14:23).*

Tim

 My Turn!

I'm happily driving along on my way to work, and then I hit it. *The intersection from hell.*

I pull up to the stop sign. Across the road, cars face me that also have a stop sign. Between us, running perpendicular (remember those algebra terms?), another road leads into town. Cars traveling on that road don't have to stop to let us in. So here I sit, waiting for an opening—my chance to turn left toward town.

This is the way it works: one car goes from the opposite side, then one from my side, one from that side, one from mine.

OK, now there's an opening. A pickup across the road comes straight across. Now it's my turn.

Hey, what's this? Another car from that side is sneaking through the intersection right behind the pickup. No fair! It's *my* turn!

I slam on the brakes. Now I'm mad. (At least I have eight minutes of driving left before I arrive at work—eight minutes to get a grip.)

You see, this isn't the first time . . . or the second time . . . or the third time I've been the victim of unfairness at this intersection. And I'm getting tired of stop-sign cheaters!

Sometimes now I just pull out when it's *my turn,* even though I spot another car sneaking across. Eventually one of us has to hit the brakes, and you know what? Usually the driver of the "cheating" car acts like it's *my* fault. (Where are cops when you *want* them?) I'm getting convinced that those vehicles coming from the other direction, those people from Smithsburg, don't get the concept of fairness.

But during those last eight minutes of driving this morning, I started thinking about fairness. I get pretty upset when things aren't fair.

Yet the Bible never promises fairness on this earth. God never says everyone will get the same treatment.

No, He says that when we do the right thing, we'll get persecuted. Good Christians will fall sick and become poor and have people take advantage of them. Life's not fair.

And you know, God doesn't even promise that His kingdom is fair. From everything I've read about Jesus and God, I don't see that They treat everybody the same.

The vineyard workers in Jesus' parable (Matthew 20:1-16) all got paid the same, even though some worked much longer than others. The prodigal son received a party when he came home, even though the other brother had hung around the whole time.

No, life's not fair. God's not fair. He doesn't say, "You give Me something; I'll give you something. Your turn, My turn." He says, "I've given everything for every one of you; just open your hands and accept it."

Actually, He unfairly gives us *all* much more than we deserve. I think I can take that kind of unfairness, can't you?

"Who is a God like you, who pardons sin and forgives the transgression of the remnant of his inheritance? You do not stay angry forever but delight to show mercy" (Micah 7:18). Lori

In Five Years I'll Be . . .

I read a statistic in a study about public school students. In any given class you attend, it's more likely that one of the students will end up in jail after graduation than that one of them will take that class subject as a major in college.

How can you avoid falling into destruction or hopelessness and instead launch into a successful life? One way to stay on track is to answer these questions:

"What do I want to be doing in five years? And how do I get there?"

You probably wouldn't say that in five years you'll be a single parent or heavily in debt or doing some time. But some people end up in these circumstances anyway. And not just adults. Teenagers too. Almost always, they did not *plan* for bad things to happen.

I've asked myself at different times, while I was still in school or at a job, "What will I do after this?" I found that two factors play a major part in keeping me on track.

Step one, ask yourself what you like and want in each area of your life. Then write it down. Consider the following questions as you do it.

What do you think is God's place in your life? What kind of person would you want to be with every day for 50 years? What kind of work would you be happy doing all week—even when you're sick and tired? Where do you like living? What kind of church experience inspires you? Who do you want to become in the coming years?

Step two is simple but not always easy. I've found that it's best to take all those answers from step one and *give them to God*. Say to Him (in your mind or out loud), "Here's what sounds good for the future. What do You think?"

Then ask Him to lead you toward what He knows will make you happy and fulfilled. He will do it in His own time.

"Those who know your name will trust in you, for you, Lord, have never forsaken those who seek you" (Psalm 9:10). *Tim*

65
Cheerleaders

OK, so I thought I was buff. I can do an hour and a half of step aerobics. And I usually walk too fast for my friends.

That's why I thought I would ace my first 5K run.

As I stood with the other runners, the announcer belted through a megaphone, "OK, let's line up. Everyone who runs a five-minute mile, come to the front. Those who do a six-minute mile, line up behind them. Next those with a seven-minute mile . . ."

I looked around. A woman in her 70s said, "Oh, I do a 10-minute mile."

Well, I guess I'll just stand with the eight-minute crowd, I thought. *I'm sure I can beat her.*

The alarm sounded, and I dashed forward. After going about 500 yards, I began to slow down. My heart was pounding, and I felt as though I couldn't get enough air into my lungs. People began to pass me.

About the time I reached the one-mile marker, I had slowed to a walk. Then I rounded a corner and saw the crowd cheering the runners on.

"Here comes Lori!" my friend Cindy shouted. "Yeah!"

"Way to go!" chanted my husband, Kim.

I picked up my pace and jogged for almost another mile, until the track led me into a back pasture. I slowed to a walk again.

But then the trail brought me back to where the crowd could see me. I spied my friends waving, and I began to run. Sweat dripped from my burning face, and my legs felt like weights, but I ran.

"Come on!" yelled Mark.

"You're winning, Lori!" my friend Charlotte teased, laughing.

"You can make it!" Kim added.

I thought I had nearly reached the finish line, but then a referee pointed to one more loop.

"I can't do it!" I gasped to Kim.

"Yes you can!" he encouraged. And then he began to run beside me. We rounded that last corner together, and I jumped over the finish line. My time: 35:47.

So I'm not buff. And no trophy sits in my office this morning.

But I learned a little about cheerleading. The friends who shouted encouragement made all the difference. Especially one who said, "I can tell this is getting hard. Let me run with you till you get there."

Is anyone around you running a tough race today? See someone sweating, straining, sore, thirsty? Try being a cheerleader!

"Let us encourage one another—and all the more as you see the Day approaching" (Hebrews 10:25).

Lori

Should You Be Witnessing?

My favorite witnessing story is the book of Jonah.

God called Jonah at home and told him to go to a big city and announce over the airwaves that God would burn the place down with everybody in it if they all didn't completely turn from their wicked ways. Jonah got out the door and ran—in the other direction.

What was Jonah thinking, anyway? Maybe he was scared. He

wasn't going to be Mr. Popularity in Nineveh. Did he have other stuff he wanted to do instead? If you really don't want to do something, everything else you could do looks so much more desirable.

Truth is, God asked Jonah to do something that he had the ability to do. Jonah just didn't want to use his unique gifts. What is God asking you to do?

You may have heard one of those sermons that lays heavy guilt on you because you haven't challenged any strangers with the gospel this week. You and I feel guilty when we hear those sermons because we assume that everyone has the same gift from God when it comes to witnessing. And we assume it's our personal responsibility to get up the courage to hammer unbelievers into being disciples. If you feel scared enough to run away to sea when faced with witnessing, you need some good advice.

You have a God-given gift you can use to fulfill the Great Commission ("Go and make disciples of all nations" [Matthew 28:19]). You may not feel naturally cozy with strangers or be able to deliver rousing sermons. But as members of Christ's body on earth—the church—each of us takes a small part in the work of the body.

So relax. Don't hide from God when He calls you. The answer to all your witnessing worries is to let Him lead you.

"Trust in the Lord with all your heart and lean not on your own understanding; in all your ways acknowledge him, and he will make your paths straight" (Proverbs 3:5, 6).

Tim

What Does Your Wallet Say?

Last Sunday my husband, Kim, and I shopped at an outlet mall near Richmond, Virginia. At a traffic light on our way out, I spotted a wallet on the ground.

"Wait!" I said, climbing out of the car. I gathered the strewn contents and jumped back in. Opening the wallet, I found a driver's license belonging to Sharon.

"She must be so worried," I said. "Poor thing!"

"Let's stop at a phone booth and call her," Kim suggested.

So we pulled over and dialed the phone number on her checkbook. It turned out to be a business number.

"I guess I'll have to try her tomorrow morning," I sighed.

"Maybe there's a home number in there," Kim offered.

So I began "snooping" through the wallet. I felt kind of uncomfortable going through a stranger's things, but also fascinated.

From her driver's license I discovered that Sharon is one year younger than I am, one inch taller, and five pounds heavier. From the business cards she carried, I guess she likes Japanese food and has friends who work for the government. She must prefer one particular airline, because she has a frequent flyer card. And she likes to buy books, because she belongs to a book club.

The last two checks Sharon wrote were to Gap Kids and the Disney Store. Her medical card said she's covered for herself and a dependent. So I think Sharon has a baby.

I never did find Sharon's home phone number, but as I looked through her papers and photos and began seeing what matters to her, I began to feel that I sort of knew her. And I liked her. She has likes and dislikes, people who are precious to her, and budgets and dreams.

This morning I called Sharon's work and told her I had found her wallet.

"I can't believe you have it!" she squealed. "Oh, there are still good people in the world. God bless you!"

She explained that she had placed her wallet on the car roof while putting her baby girl in the car seat. She forgot about it and drove away.

I packed Sharon's wallet in an envelope and couldn't resist the urge to put something encouraging in there. So I slipped in a gift copy of *The Bible Story* for her baby girl.

From Sharon's wallet I'm beginning to understand a little about how God can love each of us. He looks deep into every corner of our wallets—and our hearts. He understands us. He knows us intimately, and He loves us deeply.

And as we look at those around us and see what and who they care about, we will grow in love toward them too.

"Even the very hairs of your head are all numbered" (Matthew 10:30).

Lori

That Voice Again

Quick quiz: How many times did God speak to Jesus while Jesus was living on earth? Ten seconds is all you get. Come on, don't you remember?

OK, you can give up, because I don't know either. But the other day I found one more instance than I knew about. I love it when I read something interesting in the Bible that I've never really noticed before.

With crowds bustling all around Him, Jesus says to His disciples one day, "My heart is troubled, and what shall I say? 'Father, save me from this hour'? No, it was for this very reason I came to this hour. Father, glorify your name!" (John 12:27, 28).

Suddenly a voice booms out, "I have glorified it, and will glorify it again" (verse 28). God the Father spoke right back!

And then people in the audience reacted. Some said they heard thunder. Others said they heard an angel speak to Jesus. And Jesus immediately said, "This voice was for your benefit, not mine" (verse 30).

Now, I have a theory on this phenomenon. I think it may turn out to be true that the people who believed in Jesus and loved God heard an actual voice and real words. They thought it was an angel. I think those who *didn't* believe in Jesus and were just rubbernecking only heard thunder. What do you think?

I know that when the end of this world comes and God announces the arrival of His Son to everyone on the planet, I want to be able to hear His actual words and not just a bunch of deafening booming sounds. How about you?

"A time is coming and has now come when the dead will hear the voice of the Son of God and those who hear will live" (John 5:25).

Tim

License to . . .

My grandmother is 93 years old. She called me yesterday to tell me that they took away her driver's license.

You see, Grandma had gone to the Department of Motor Vehicles to get her license renewed. But they took her old one and didn't give her a new one.

In her heavy German accent she explained what she did wrong during her driving test (according to the driving inspector): "I didn't turn my head at one street. I *knew* no one was coming!"

Grandma continued, "And the inspector said to me, 'You can't make your signs.' "

"What?" I asked her. "You mean hand signals?"

"Yes!" Grandma exclaimed. "We made those signs 60 years ago! Now we have everything inside the car—signals and lights. Why do we have to make signs out the window?"

She's got a point, don't you think?

I feel bad for Grandma because this is a real blow to her. She has a car, and she can't drive it anymore. "When things go like this," she said to me, "you feel very old and ready to die."

I thought about how many of you are just *getting* your driver's licenses. And I thought about how Grandma is *losing* hers.

And I guess I just have this to say: When you're out there on the road and you see someone like my grandma—someone older who's maybe driving slower than you'd like, or not like you learned to drive—be patient. Because driving means as much to them as it does to you.

"Show respect for the elderly and revere your God" (Leviticus 19:32).

Lori

That's Cold, Baby

Seventeen-year-old Mike Wright thought he'd found the easy ride. By hopping a freight train, he figured he could get a free trip into Crofton, the town nearest his home in western Kentucky.

But the train passed Crofton and stopped in Evansville, Indiana, 65 miles away. So Wright jumped out and climbed into an insulated produce car he thought was headed back toward Crofton—and home.

But he fell asleep and later woke up to find that someone had latched the door. And the train was still rolling.

A week and 2,000 miles later two railroad workers in Hermiston, Oregon, heard Wright calling for help and let him out. One of the workers said Wright couldn't walk straight but had a big smile on his face. He was treated at a hospital for dehydration.

A railroad spokesman pointed out that though the refrigeration was turned off, the insulation had kept the boxcar cool and kept Mike Wright alive. This kind of accident often ends in death. (Adapted from Associated Press news release, August 23, 1995. Used by permission.)

If Wright had known where he would end up, would he have gone ahead with what he did? I don't think so.

Now, I'm not going to tell you that you shouldn't do this and you shouldn't do that because you'll end up dead in a boxcar. But I know a way to find out exactly where we're going.

Because He's completely smart and knows everything, God can show us the outcomes of our choices. He's on our side, and He's not keeping any secrets when it comes to our happiness. So anytime you're ready to launch into a choice with an uncertain outcome, check with God and ask Him to light the way. He's waiting for you to ask so that He can work for you.

"Do you know how the clouds hang poised, those wonders of him who is perfect in knowledge?" (Job 37:16).

Tim

7
"I'm Choking!"

Recently I read a great story in a news magazine. This is what happened.

Employees and guests at St. Helena Hospital and Health Center in California had gathered in the cafeteria to eat their lunches. Suddenly a man started choking on his sandwich.

The person with him jumped up and began performing the Heimlich maneuver on him. But the man continued choking.

Then Carolyn Craig, a young nurse at the hospital, stepped in. She wrapped her arms around the man's body and began putting pressure on his diaphragm. She says she remembered the training video she'd watched in nursing school. "Sometimes you have to repeat the maneuver six to 10 times," she said to herself.

Carolyn repeated the procedure *nine* times. She began to say to herself, "This isn't going to work!" But on the *tenth* attempt, the food was dislodged, and the man could breathe normally again.

A few days later Henry J. Heimlich, M.D., *the* developer of the Heimlich maneuver, visited St. Helena Hospital for a program. Carolyn got to meet him.

"Thank you for the maneuver," she said.

"Thank you for using it," he replied.

That story made me think a lot. You know, we're pretty lucky to know about God. We read the Bible and learn His character and become friends with Jesus, our Saviour. We see the commandments for living happy, fulfilled lives. We go to church and learn more every week about good living and how to share that news with our friends.

We *have* the Heimlich maneuver for not choking in this violent, poisonous world.

But do we *use* it? A saving procedure doesn't do any good if it doesn't get used.

Let's not just say we know the ticket to living right. Let's use it.

"Not everyone who says to me, 'Lord, Lord,' will enter the kingdom of heaven, but only he who does the will of my Father who is in heaven" (Matthew 7:21).

Lori

I'm Not Suffering—Yet

Even though I'm over 30 now, I've never had a serious illness. In fact, I've never stayed in a hospital, and only have had to go to the emergency room once (I hit my face with a pickax). And I've never been in a car wreck. Not even a fender bender.

I've prayed for people with life-threatening diseases and others who have been in bad auto accidents, but I don't know what it's like to be in their shoes. I guess I feel a little guilty sometimes because so many people have suffering in their lives and I don't.

In the office building where I work, a group of employees gets together at least once a week and prays for specific people with needs that we want to present to God. There's a teen in Tasmania, Australia, who has cancer; a Miss Texas Coed winner whose doctors can't figure out what's making her sick; a family whose young daughter was murdered recently. Wow, these people need major power from the Lord to get through their suffering!

Didn't Jesus say, "Go into your room, close the door and pray to your Father, who is unseen. Then your Father, who sees what is done in secret, will reward you" (Matthew 6:6)?

But didn't He also say, "Your Father knows what you need before you ask him" (verse 8)? Could He maybe be saying that God knows everything but He wants us to ask anyway?

I've figured a couple good reasons to ask God to heal and encourage other people. One is that an 18-year-old guy with cancer may be too discouraged to pray for himself. He may think God has given up on him or isn't listening. We can ask God to go to him and lift him out of the dumps so he can face his tragedy.

The other reason is that we become aware of the gift of good health. Just in the past month I've begun to thank God for each *day* of healthy, energetic living, because tomorrow I may join the ranks of the afflicted.

Praying for the needs of others helps them and us, so you might want to get in on this win/win situation. Just get down on your knees behind a closed door.

"Confess your sins to each other and pray for each other so that you may be healed. The prayer of a righteous man is powerful and effective" (James 5:16).

Tim

Up, Up, and Away

I caught a late-night flight last week from St. Louis back to Maryland. When I found my seat and saw that the plane wasn't very full, I was glad, because I wanted to sleep.

But then a mother and her three sons (approximate ages: 3, 4, and 5) came down the aisle and took the row in front of me—on both sides of the plane. One boy sat next to her and the other two settled into seats across the aisle from her.

Boy, she has her hands full! I thought. *And I bet I won't be able to sleep now. They'll probably be loud. Maybe I can move to another row after the plane takes off.*

But by the time we got off the ground, I didn't *want* to move. These kids were more entertaining than a movie!

This was obviously their first plane ride, and they were excited. They immediately began to explore: they turned the lights above their seats on and off, pushed the call button (the flight attendant was patient), put their meal tray up and down, pushed the window shades up and down, and fastened and unfastened their seat belts.

Their mother finally convinced them that they had to stay in their seats with their belts fastened until they saw the seat belt light go off. As the plane squealed down the runway for takeoff, the 4-year-old looked at his brothers and said, "It's like a squeeeeeky mouse."

Then, during the flight, the 3-year-old stood on his chair and craned his neck to look out the window. Suddenly he pointed and shouted with a big grin, "Mommy, a white pillow in the sky!"

Near the end of the flight one looked out the window and shouted, "I saw *buildings!"* like that was the most exciting thing in the universe.

As the plane landed—just as it touched the ground—they began shouting, "Daddy! Daddy! Daddy!" And they pushed their way down the aisle and ran into their father's arms at the arrival gate.

As I watched the boys tell their dad all about their plane ride, I thought about our heavenly Father and about the trip we'll take one day to see Him and His kingdom.

Right now it's so hard for Him to help us understand what it's like—and what He's like. Like those little boys who had never flown before, we just can't relate. We have to use earthly images like mice and pillows and fathers.

But one day we'll take the trip into eternity. And I have a feeling that no matter how foreign things look to us, we'll still shout "Daddy!" when we get to that golden gate. We'll know Him, because He's been walking with us all along.

"How great is the love the Father has lavished on us, that we should be called children of God! And that is what we are!" (1 John 3:1).

Lori

It's Just Temptation

I haven't eaten all day. Somehow I never found the time. I'm absolutely starving, and I would eat any food that didn't have little things *growing* on it.

Then my buddy Tompaul comes into the office and says, "Imagine this. A five-scoop ice-cream boat—chocolate-chip cookie dough, strawberry cheesecake, chocolate mint chip, pralines and cream, and lime sherbet—covered with hot caramel, chopped walnuts, multicolored sprinkles, banana slices, fake whipped cream, and three cherries. Wouldn't that do it for you?"

I need nutrition. *I want ice cream.*

Oscar Wilde once said, "I can resist everything except temptation."

How do you deal with temptations? Check out these points:

1. The temptations you meet up with, whether shooting heroin or playing hooky, having sex or sassing teachers, do not come from God. He doesn't tempt anyone. The Bible says, "When tempted, no one should say, 'God is tempting me.' For God cannot be tempted by evil, nor does he tempt anyone" (James 1:13).

2. We have various destructive desires inside us, and we can either pursue them or give them to God. "Each one is tempted when, by his own evil desire, he is dragged away and enticed" (verse 14). If you're listening to your conscience, it will tell you that the desire is wrong, no matter how good it looks.

3. All the temptations you face have no effect unless you allow them to give birth to an actual act. "After desire has conceived, it gives birth to sin; and sin, when it is full-grown, gives birth to death" (verse 15). So having temptations does not put you over the edge, but acting on them will take you down.

4. You may want what you're tempted by, but you have to weigh that against the consequences. If you give in to a destructive desire,

you're pushing God away. You're saying, "Thanks, God, but no thanks. I'm going my way." And that, in the end, means destruction and death.

5. What's the up side here? God is there to help you. Alcoholics Anonymous keeps people from the temptation of alcohol because it points them to a higher power. You can't do it alone, but help is there for the taking. For the little temptations and the big ones, go to God.

"The wages of sin is death, but the gift of God is eternal life in Christ Jesus our Lord" (Romans 6:23).

Tim

Risky Business

Which on this list would you consider the most "risky" for you?

a. going bungee jumping
b. asking a senior to be your date at the school banquet
c. offering prayer out loud in youth group
d. eating a grasshopper
e. telling friends you don't drink or want to
f. feeding the homeless in an inner city
g. swimming across the deep end of the pool
h. going to the mall in your pajamas
i. walking out of a raunchy movie or turning off a video
j. visiting someone with AIDS
k. going to a party where you don't know anyone
l. talking to a stranger about Jesus

Do you think we should take risks? Does God want us to—or not want us to?

I'm not a real courageous person, so I kinda hoped I could serve God from the soft safety of home. But as I began to look through the Bible, I found that *every* Bible hero—and every person even mentioned as a follower of God—took risks. Some took big-time major ones.

Take Noah. Talk about peer pressure. He had to stand out in a public place and build a huge ark for years while everyone else stood around and made fun of him.

What about Moses? When God called him to lead the children of Israel, Moses said, "O Lord, I have never been eloquent. . . . I am slow of speech and tongue. . . . Please send someone else to do it" (Exodus 4:10-13). But God challenged Moses to take the risk, and came through to help him.

And check out Gideon in Judges 7. God kept telling him to make his army smaller and smaller, till his force was completely outnumbered by the enemy. But with God's help he won the battle!

Speaking of battles . . . What about the ultimate unfair fight? David and giant Goliath. Now, that was a risky situation.

And Esther. She kind of entered a beauty pageant for God and His people. Major risk for me, anyway.

Then Daniel, praying in public when he was told not to. And ending up in a lions' den.

Mary, the mother of Jesus. What a risk she took in carrying God's child! Talk about people whispering behind your back and not believing you. (Would you feel comfortable telling people that an angel visited you and gave you that awesome responsibility?)

Then there's Mary Magdalene, who risked leaving her old habits and familiar sins when Jesus challenged her to.

And Jesus. If anyone took a big risk, He did. He had *everything* to lose. Yet He risked it all for us.

From reading the Bible, I get the message that God asks us to take risks for Him. Not just foolish, adrenaline-flow risks. But *redemptive* risks for His kingdom. There's a difference.

Check out this text. Paul is writing to the Philippians about a guy named Epaphroditus. He says the guy was sick, but is now well and coming back to Philippi. "Welcome him in the Lord with great joy," Paul instructs, "and honor men like him, because he almost died for the work of Christ" (Philippians 2:29, 30).

Now check out this statement by William Barclay: "There should be in the Christian an almost reckless courage which makes him ready to gamble with his life to serve Christ and men" *(The Letters to the Philippians, Colossians, and Thessalonians,* Daily Study Bible Series, revised edition, p. 50).

Jesus promised that if we lay down our lives, we'll find them. Yeah, following God is risky, but it's a safe bet.

"Who is going to harm you if you are eager to do good? But even if you should suffer for what is right, you are blessed. 'Do not fear what they fear; do not be frightened.' But in your hearts set apart Christ as Lord" (1 Peter 3:13-15).

Lori

Lighten Up

Whatever you do this week, don't forget to smile. You think I'm joking. Hey, I'm serious. You really have no reason not to. In fact, I think it should be a federal law. OK, now I am kidding. Here's what I think you should do and why.

Smile at someone you walk by in the mall or at church or on campus or wherever. There are right and wrong ways to do this.

You do have to look at the person, but don't stare. If you look at them and they look at you but they don't seem hostile or insulted because you're looking at them, give them a grin.

If you look at them and they look unhappy, as though they're thinking *What IS he staring at?* give them a quick flash of the pearls and then look away. No one will shoot you for that.

If they look away when you look at them, smile anyway. It's not as if you can waste a smile or anything.

If you usually don't smile at anybody, start small. Try it on one person you know. When (surprise) they don't hit you or stare or fall down, you'll gain confidence that you can smile at a complete stranger and live to tell about it.

A word of caution, though, because the real world is, well, you know, the real world. Smiling at people has never gotten me into any trouble. But I'm a guy, so I can't really say that smiling at all kinds of strangers is good for girls to do. Use your common sense here. For instance, you might not want to do it when you're alone.

So why do this? It will tell you quickly whether you accept all people as children of God or are actually harboring some kind of prejudice against some of them. It might be racial prejudice. But it's more likely to be "they're-different-from-me" prejudice or "they-don't-look-like-my-type" bias.

You can't reject people you smile at. Believe me. I've tried.

"I will forget my complaint, I will change my expression, and smile" (taken out of context from Job 9:27).

Tim

Rated Reject

When's the last time you've seen a good video? Now, when I say "good," I mean *good.*

My husband, Kim, and I have rented some real losers lately. First we rented something we knew would get our adrenaline going. We'd heard great reviews on it.

We turned it off halfway through. I got tired of holding my hands over my face, and Kim said, "We don't need to watch this."

The next time we went to the video store, we determined to rent something that wouldn't scare or offend us.

We were right. It didn't. It just bored us.

We turned that one off too.

Last Saturday night some friends began to tell us about awful videos they'd seen lately and regretted. One had been at the house of some other friends.

That's when I made some decisions:

1. I'm going to turn off videos when they seem inappropriate for a Christian—or when they are a boring waste of time.

I know friends who give videos the "Christ" test: "If Jesus were here with me, would I feel comfortable watching this video with Him?" (Hey, I'm uncomfortable watching most videos with my parents!) Give videos the "Christ" test, and you'll set some good, high standards.

2. I'm not going to expose my friends to a video unless I'm sure it's good in every way. (That won't leave me much to show, will it?)

3. I'm going to explore the Christian video market. A few years ago I had no idea what awesome Christian music I could get at a Christian bookstore. Maybe it's the same for Christian videos.

Are you ready to rate some videos "**R**ejected" and search for only the "**G**ood"?

"Whatever is true, whatever is noble, whatever is right, whatever is pure, whatever is lovely, whatever is admirable— if anything is excellent or praiseworthy—think about such things" (Philippians 4:8).

Lori

Fooled You

I hate being tricked. I'd march into class at school, and something wet and slimy would drop on my head as I walked through the door. Everyone would laugh. Head down, I'd just keep going. Call me insecure, but it really got to me.

The year before I came to work at *Insight* I gave a tour of the building where I was working. A group of Rotarians from England wanted to see what an Adventist publishing house does. None of them knew much about Adventists or even about the Bible or Christianity.

One of the Rotarians, a police officer, asked straight out, "So what makes Adventists different from other Christian groups?"

"Uh, well . . . ah," I said, having no answer ready, "we believe the end of the world is coming and so we want to warn people about it, and we think Saturday is still God's day of worship."

"Hmmm. Oh. I see," the Rotarians said.

That was it. Not wanting to hammer them with our doctrines, I didn't say more, and they didn't ask more.

Was I ready? No. You might say those Rotarians tricked me. I was in the middle of a situation before I found out how much I didn't know.

I hate that feeling of not knowing what I need to know in order to handle a situation. All my life I've heard and learned what Adventist Christians believe. But if the knowledge just sits there, it's just taking up space in my head. I have to prepare ahead of time to be ready to pass on the knowledge to others.

When Jesus said, "Be as shrewd as snakes and as innocent as doves" (Matthew 10:16), He meant, "Don't be naive. Know what you're getting into. And don't do any wrong." It's time for us to get ready.

"Whoever acknowledges me before men, I will also acknowledge him before my Father in heaven" (Matthew 10:32).

The Lion, the White Sale, and My Wardrobe

Right now I'm waiting for the phone to ring. And since I'm having a hard time thinking about anything else, I've decided I'll tell you about this phone call I'm waiting for.

You see, I visited my parents recently for Christmas, and my mom and sister and grandma and I (three generations) hit the day-after-Christmas sales.

Let's just say I hit it big. A dress. Three tops. Two pairs of jeans. Two pairs of shorts. A wool vest. Two sweaters. A pantsuit. All on major sale.

Well, flying back, the airline lost my hanging bag. Right. The bag with all the new clothes in it. They said they'll call me when they find it. They told me my clothes could be in Houston, Texas. Or Kansas City. Or Milwaukee. Or Cleveland. Or Newark. Or I guess (and I don't think they want to mention this) the bag could have been stolen.

Before going on vacation I was talking to Tim, who said he's not into clothes a whole lot. Well, I *am*. And I have to admit I'm not real proud about the fact that I'm so worried about a bag of clothes.

I mean, it's not like I don't have anything else to wear. I don't really *need* those things. (So why, you ask, did I buy them?)

Good question.

And why am I so upset about losing them?

Good question.

I just looked in *The Clear Word* paraphrase and found some words by Jesus to help me handle this loss. Here's what it says:

"If God makes the flowers of the field so beautiful when they last only until someone mows them down and throws them into the fire, don't you think He cares much more about providing your physical needs? Why do you have such little faith in Him?

131

"Stop being so concerned about what to eat and drink.

"That's what unbelievers worry about. But you have a Father who loves you and knows that you need those things" (Luke 12:28-30, Clear Word).

Sounds like I'm acting like an unbeliever, doesn't it? God takes care of me, but I want more, more, more.

Maybe my bag will show up. Maybe it won't. But if I keep spending time with God's Word, maybe I'll find out that it doesn't really matter.

"Do not worry about your life, what you will eat; or about your body, what you will wear. Life is more than food, and the body more than clothes" (Luke 12:22, 23)

Lori

Still in the Minefield

A number of *Insight* readers wrote in a recent survey last spring that they hadn't made a commitment to God or the church yet because they were still searching. I'm glad that those of you who have questions about the truth are looking for your own answers.

Maybe I can help a little. I read a statement the other day that went something like this: The gospel is not a debate or a discussion; it's an announcement.

What's the announcement? God has made it possible for every person to escape this imperfect world and live with Him in a perfect, happy world.

Radical claim, huh? The question you face is Is it true?

While you're gathering evidence and experience to help you decide, consider a few observations I've made about the way things are.

First, no human being has been able to promise happiness and actually follow through with it. Nor has any impersonal agent like nature, science, money, or peanut M&Ms. Which leaves the possibility that God can.

Second, the devil is ultimately responsible for every bad thing in earth's history (although he's been aided by plenty of human followers). God and the devil have been at war since the rebellion in heaven, and we're still sitting in the devil's territory right now.

Third, God has told us what the reward is for being patient through the suffering and injustice of life here. And He's giving us the reward simply for believing that we can have it. Because when we believe His promise, we're telling God we can trust Him.

Have you heard someone say that Jesus suffered more from the pain of having the entire population's sins loaded on Him than from the pain of being nailed to a piece of wood? You can believe it. And because Jesus carried that huge burden to His death, you can drop your heavy load and grab on to His announcement with air under your wings.

"John saw Jesus coming toward him and said, 'Look, the Lamb of God, who takes away the sin of the world!'" (John 1:29).

My Homeless Friend

One Christmas break I volunteered on an urban mission project in Los Angeles, California. On the van heading to the food bank, I met Cheri Peters, who shared her story with our group.

Cheri was homeless from ages 13 to 23. Her mother got pregnant with Cheri when she was 14. She didn't want her, so Cheri grew up knowing only hate and abuse, first from her father and then from her mother's next husband, who was an alcoholic.

I guess you can understand why Cheri left home and ended up on the streets. Once there, she got adopted by a group of addicts and dealers who used her to move shipments of cocaine.

"You don't see kids and teenagers on the streets very much," she told our group. "That's because they've been picked up by perpetrators and drug addicts who will use them till they're used up."

She warned, "When you hear friends say 'I'll just run away,' you have no idea what that means."

One day Cheri told a guy in a bar, "I'm a mess. I'm addicted to everything, and I don't know what to do."

He replied, "I have a sister in Placerville; you can rehab in her house."

When Cheri walked into the sister's home, the woman said, "I want you to know I love you."

Cheri wasn't used to hearing that, and she didn't believe the woman. After all, this woman was a strict Seventh-day Adventist, very different from Cheri. Cheri decided to prove her a fake.

She began telling the woman the most shocking things she'd ever done. The woman would listen, sometimes crying, sometimes running to the bathroom in the middle of a story. Later she told Cheri that she would go there and pray, "God, help me to love this woman. Help me not to judge her."

God's love finally broke through to Cheri, and she accepted Him as her Saviour.

She told our group, "When you do missionary work, remember that God is working really hard for those people on the streets. When you smile at them and look them in the eye, they will wonder, *Why in the world do you love me?* All you have to do is love them, and the Holy Spirit will take it from there."

"A new command I give you: Love one another. As I have loved you, so you must love one another. By this all men will know that you are my disciples, if you love one another" (John 13:34, 35, Lori

Hold the Phone

I see similarities between your school schedule and the one I try to keep on *Insight*. As the weeks rush by, I have to get some work done and hand some stuff in. Sound familiar?

The biggest difference between your schedule and mine is that I don't have homework. Ha ha ha ha. Sorry. One day yours will end. Perhaps after high school. Or college.

Anyway, after a few weeks I get so busy doing busywork that I'm running with my nose near the dirt and can't think straight anymore. So I have to stop and assess my progress.

I have a bad habit of starting a project and then starting another one and then another one. Each one sits on top of the last. This past week I couldn't find the pen I usually write with or a phone number I needed—danger signs that important things had been buried on my desk. Who knows what's lurking in the mess.

So I stopped everything and took inventory: What projects did I need to finish? What should my priorities be?

Even though the Bible tells us to take one day at a time, we seem to have an internal clock that doesn't match up with the 24-hour day. Some days I'm running on fast forward and get lots of articles read and edited. Other days I can't seem to get off pause. Several hours go by, and I look back and think, *What have I gotten done?*

One way around this time dilemma is to make realistic goals. Instead of plotting out what you're going to do every hour, try setting goals for the day and for the week. If you have a history paper due next week, commit to three afternoons for research and two for writing it.

Also, be brutal about what your highest priorities are. Shooting baskets, talking on the phone, or watching TV shouldn't be at the top!

Finally, we won't make progress unless we take spiritual inventory quite often. I find that I have to let God control me in everything I do

135

because I'm the kind of person who gets bugged over little, stupid stuff. So if I forget about God's influence (which happens at least a couple times a day), I have to stop what I'm doing and let God slap up my attitude.

"Reverence for the Lord is the foundation of knowledge. People are fools who refuse to listen to Him" (Proverbs 1:7, Clear Word).

Tim

83
Describe Me

"The person in the white T-shirt, your pump is ready," came the voice over the loudspeaker.

I pressed on the nozzle and began to pump gasoline into my Honda Civic. As I pumped I listened to other people getting the go-ahead through the convenience store loudspeaker.

"The man in the jean shorts, your pump is ready."

"The person in the red Pinto, your pump is ready."

"The man in the—um—orange tank top, your pump is ready."

The next time I went to the station, I again waited for the attendant to give me the OK to begin pumping.

"The blond-haired lady in the flowered shorts with the green shirt and the white tennis shoes and white socks, your pump is ready."

I looked down at what I was wearing. Sure enough, the person got the whole description right. Then I looked over at the store to see who had described me in such detail. I couldn't even see the person. How did they see me so well?

I laughed as I listened to the attendant give the OK to the next customer. "The man in the 501s with the Hard Rock Café T-shirt, cowboy boots, and beard, your pump is ready."

Evidently the person at the microphone was trying to add a little interest to his job!

The next time I stopped in I asked someone behind the counter to tell me their policy in describing customers.

"We don't have a policy," the woman responded with a shrug. "I just pick something that sticks out to me, like a blue shirt."

Then the manager got into the conversation. "We try to train the people the right way—they shouldn't get too creative, 'cause people do take offense," he said. "Sometimes we can't see the person physically, so we authorize the car, but we like to authorize the person."

"What do you mean, people take offense?" I asked.

"Well, sometimes it's hard to tell the difference between a Dodge Caravan and a Plymouth Voyager," he explained with a laugh. "People don't like it if you call their vehicle the wrong thing."

"Any funny stories?" I probed.

The manager smiled. "One time I was working in the back, and I heard the guy say over the loudspeaker, 'The gentleman with the magic bus, your pump is ready.' I had to come out and see what that was."

"What was it?" I wanted to know.

"It was an old school bus that the guy had made into a camper. My attendant said he just froze and didn't know what to say, so he just called it a magic bus."

"Has an attendant ever said the wrong thing and gotten fired?" I continued.

"No," the manager replied. "Sometimes you start saying one thing and then you think, *Uh-oh—that might offend.* So you say something else. We try not to be too descriptive, 'cause people do take offense at how they're addressed."

As I drove away, I heard words coming over the loudspeaker: "The man in the brown shorts . . . The person in the beige Mustang . . ."

I thought about the manager's last statement and began to wonder if we ever choose to get to know—or not get to know—someone based on one thing that sticks out to us. Are we ever as shallow about our friendships as the person running the loudspeaker at the gas station?

I hope not. I'd like to be more than "the person in the white T-shirt." Wouldn't you?

"The Lord does not look at the things man looks at. Man looks at the outward appearance, but the Lord looks at the heart" (1 Samuel 16:7).

Lori

Hey, We're Family

You probably have relatives who are not Adventists. Maybe they're not Christians at all. So they like pork chops and coffee, Friday nights on the town, Saturday morning cartoons, maybe beer and cigarettes.

I have my share of non-Adventist relatives, and all my life I've encountered situations that I wasn't sure how to handle. Perhaps you've encountered this too. You know, you're visiting your great-aunt, and she puts a plate of sliced brownish-gray meat product on the table and encourages you to dive in. She's been on your parents' prayer list for decades, so you don't want to say "Eww, yech, that stuff's unclean!" But you're a meat virgin and not about to give in now.

And you've got a visiting cousin who wants to watch TV all Friday evening, and another who collects *Playgirl,* and one who drinks too much vodka on the weekends. Or your uncle watches a sex-and-violence flick on cable, and you don't want to be rude and walk out, but you feel you should.

It may be closer to you than that. My brother is not an Adventist, although you couldn't find a nicer guy. He doesn't know what it's like to know God and have Him light up your life. But my brother means a great deal to me, and I'm not sure I should try to show him how much by trying to force him back into the church. It brings me back to the basic problem: how to act toward non-Adventist family.

I think the answer lies in two types of prayer. If you find yourself pressured by a family member to do something you don't believe is right, pray immediately. Say, "God, help! Please tell me what to say and what to do." God said to us in Matthew 7:8: "Everyone who asks receives." Right then is the time to put the promise to the test. This is defensive prayer.

Because of something I heard in a sermon recently, I realized that there is also offensive prayer. That same promise in Matthew 7 challenges us to seek and find, to knock and have the door opened.

Those of us who have given our allegiance to God and stepped into the light of His ways have a burden that all of our family members will find the same wonderful experience. God says, "Pray for it." He says, "Ask Me to influence their minds, to call their thoughts toward Me." And He will do it.

"I pray . . . that the eyes of your heart may be enlightened in order that you may know the hope to which he has called you, the riches of his glorious inheritance in the saints, and his incomparably great power for us who believe" (Ephesians 1:18, 19). Tim

Go for Inner Beauty

I read an article recently about what attracts guys to girls. The writer had taken nationwide polls, interviewed guys, and drawn up her statistics. And she discovered that hands down, men find women most attractive if they are warm and uncritical. Many said they would happily marry a warm and loving woman even if she didn't have perfect measurements and couldn't boil an egg.

The article convinced me even more that it's our inner beauty that counts the most. And you know, in spite of today's makeup and fashion secrets, there's still more you can do about changing your inner appearance than changing your outer appearance. In the long run, that's what matters most anyway—to other people and to God. Inner beauty is what will make you, ultimately, most beautiful and loved.

I spoke with some guys and girls about what they think makes inner beauty. And I read what the Bible has to say about it (it has a lot more to say about inner beauty than outer beauty). Here are some qualities of a beautiful person:

Warm and loving. See 1 Corinthians 13 for a full definition of love. Also read Proverbs 15:17 and Ephesians 5:1, 2.

Patient. This means being slow to lose your temper, quarrel, and especially criticize. Read Proverbs 15:18; 16:32; 21:9; 22:24; and 25:15.

Sensitive and understanding. This means being perceptive to others' hurts and joys. And it means unselfishly being able to see another's point of view. Start with Proverbs 13:15; 16:21.

Energetic and self-disciplined. This is a person who isn't afraid to work hard (not lazy). It also means showing enthusiasm. See Proverbs 13:4; 31:13-19, 27.

Cheerful. Read Ephesians 5:15, 19, 20; Proverbs 17:22; 31:25. Being happy and lighthearted is contagious (and attractive).

Loyal. A loyal person won't gossip about friends. He will stick by you and accept you no matter what. See Proverbs 11:13; 17:17.

Honest. Lying destroys trust. An honest, trustworthy person is a valuable friend. See Proverbs 17:20 and Ephesians 5:9.

Humble. Pride isn't attractive in even the most physically attractive people. A person focused on others rather than herself or himself makes the most beautiful impression. Read Proverbs 13:10; 15:32, 33; 16:5; 22:4; 25:27.

Wise. See Proverbs 13:14; 14:6-8; 15:2, 20; 25:12; 31:26. Wisdom isn't only school knowledge but common sense and an understanding of God's laws. Being able to give good advice is a great quality.

Courageous. Standing up for what's right requires courage. Showing kindness and caring toward the socially unaccepted takes courage too. See Proverbs 14:21; 31:20.

Forgiving. It's hard to forgive when you've been really hurt. But people who easily forgive others (and themselves) are free of grudges, hate, and defensiveness. Read Proverbs 15:4; Matthew 6:14, 15; 18:23-35.

A friend of God. Proverbs 31:30 and Ephesians 5:3-5 tell more about what this means.

Want to be attractive? Get into God's Word, and find the keys.

"Charm is deceptive, and beauty is fleeting; but a woman who fears the Lord is to be praised" (Proverbs 31:30).   *Lori*

Wrapped in Love

P eople have given me so many things this year.

I sat on a bench in a mall in Baltimore one day and complained to my wife about a headache. A mall employee in overalls was standing nearby emptying an ashtray stand. He must have overheard my whining, because he pulled a package out of his pocket and offered me an aspirin. He gave me the gift of relief.

Another time I walked up to the register in County Market with a 40-pound bag of dog munchies on my shoulder. The man in front of me said, "You go ahead," and stepped around me. I wanted to pay him for being so nice. He gave me his spot, no questions asked.

A couple of weeks ago I bought some cereal and chocolate chips at Martin's grocery store. After adding up the prices, I thought I had enough dollars in my pocket to cover them. But I came up 30 cents short.

Kind of embarrassed, I said to the cashier, "I'll run across to the bank for cash."

She said, "Don't worry," and pulled out a generic dollar-off coupon, ran it through with my dollars, and *gave me the change.*

I shouldn't be so surprised that God still works in the lives of many people of all ages, backgrounds, and races. He's given some people a gift for giving. They don't just buy gifts and wrap them. They see opportunities to give of themselves, and they deliver.

I want to match their gifts by passing on the blessing to others. How about you?

"So in everything, do to others as you would have them do to you, for this sums up the Law and the Prophets" (Matthew 7:12).

Tim

Follow the Leader

Who has let you down lately? A parent? A teacher? A pastor? A friend? A government official?

Chances are that some leader in your life has disappointed you. Your favorite teacher has had an extramarital affair. The pastor who baptized you has left the ministry. Your parents cheated on a business deal. The president of your class got drunk at a party. The president of the United States lied.

Those kinds of things don't make you have a lot of faith in leaders. And that's OK, except that I've seen people stop trusting *anyone.*

And because a human leader disappointed them, they've left a church or a school or a job.

That's sad. It's even sadder when people stop believing in anything but themselves.

Maybe we can't trust human leaders. But maybe we're a bit unfair to them too.

I grew up a pastor's kid, and I didn't like it when people expected me to act a certain way or to be a leader in an area I felt *I* needed leading in.

We all have weaknesses. We've all made mistakes, too. But sometimes we've just been fortunate enough not to be found out. Or since we weren't a leader, our mistakes didn't affect anyone else or become public. Leaders have to carry the burden of knowing that their failings will hurt a lot of people.

It's sometimes scary to be a leader. And it's sometimes scary to believe in leaders, especially when we see them fail again and again.

But let's look at Christ and how He handled poor leadership. He had to face bad political *and* bad spiritual leaders. The Romans were ruling the Jews during His lifetime, and much of the pain Christ encountered stemmed from conditions they caused. The leaders of the Sanhedrin were also acting in ways Christ didn't approve of.

And what did He do? He spoke to and changed everyone who would let Him. When leaders like Nicodemus, Jairus, and the rich young ruler came to Christ, He tried to help them. And when leaders of the day finally beat Him and hung Him on a cross, He forgave them *before they even asked.*

Christ also went about meeting people, trying to counteract the effects of poor leadership. He listened to what troubled them. He stopped their pain. He talked to them about His kingdom.

He changed people's perceptions of leadership. He built trust. And through His life He let them know how liberating it is to believe in Him.

So how do we know which leaders to follow? We can watch the ones who are following *the Leader.*

"Now we ask you, brothers, to respect those who work hard among you, who are over you in the Lord and who admonish you.

143

Hold them in the highest regard in love because of their work. Live in peace with each other" (1 Thessalonians 5:12, 13). *Lori*

Netiquette in Cyberspace

I think you can live and die without turning on a computer and still say you had a good life. But these days most people use a computer for something. And now that computers do more than talk back at you, you can become involved in online communication with people all around the world.

A couple in Texas used their connection to the Internet to send an advertisement for their legal services company. They "spammed" the network. (You know what happens when the spam hits the fan. It goes everywhere.)

Their ad showed up on every bulletin board on the net, totaling about 5,500 altogether. Sounds OK, unless you know what kind of people tap into the Internet.

Thousands of them, millions even, were very angry that someone would post an unwanted commercial ad on everyone's bulletin boards without so much as a "May we?"

How did these angry people react? They sent "flames" over the Internet to this lawyer couple. "Flames" are harassment strategies to bother people who break Internet etiquette ("netiquette").

Hundreds and then thousands of people began dumping long, rude, and crude messages into the couple's e-mail box, causing the e-mail server to crash repeatedly. Hundreds of others made thousands of phony requests for information. Some began sending the couple's address in for phony magazine subscriptions.

When the couple told the New York *Times* that they would advertise again, the harassment started again, this time with hundreds of blank pages sent to their fax machine and more bogus magazine subscriptions.

When Christians meet up with unrepentant people like that couple, they look to Jesus for an example. Did Jesus harass the rich young guy who turned down the opportunity to give everything away for God's sake? No, Jesus let him go without a word.

Sure, Jesus called the Pharisees some ripe names, because they were unrepentant hypocrites. But Jesus never abused anyone. He may have begged people to change, but He never lifted a finger to make their lives more miserable than they already were. He only wanted to build them up.

You may see people who need correcting, who are apathetic or hypocritical or just plain wrong. Promise yourself that you'll judge them through the eyes of Jesus.

"I tell you that men will have to give account on the day of judgment for every careless word they have spoken. For by your words you will be acquitted, and by your words you will be condemned" (Matthew 12:36, 37).

Tim

Princess

I still think about Princess Diana sometimes. I remember getting up in the dark predawn to watch her wedding. The majestic music, the beautiful princess in white, the carriage that took Diana and her prince away after the ceremony . . . I observed it all with a full heart and a big sigh.

Then I read magazine articles about Diana, and I thought that if I had grown up with her, we would probably be friends. Maybe that was unrealistic, but I'd say, "Wow, she likes swimming and jet-skiing. So do I."

I'd read another article and say, "She likes to shop. So do I. Wouldn't it be fun to go shopping together?"

Then I'd hear that she tried to work out regularly in the gym, and I'd imagine us going to step aerobics class together.

She liked to travel, and so do I. She liked people, and so do I.

When I heard about her death, I felt loss. I cried some, and I watched hours of footage from her funeral day. And I read more magazine articles about her.

But this time I noticed different things. This time I noticed that Diana had been dating a rather irresponsible guy. (Articles said that Dodi had left unpaid debts and abandoned a string of girlfriends, including one fiancée, to date Diana.) A few magazines also talked about how Diana had often visited an astrologer.

That's when I began to feel especially sad that Diana and I hadn't been friends. If we had been, I could have told her that despite the pain of an unfaithful husband and a shattered fairy tale, God had a better plan for her than an untrustworthy boyfriend. And she didn't have to turn to astrologers; God wanted to give her the desires of her heart and lead her in the path of righteous happiness.

I wish I could have told Diana about God's plan and His kingdom.

Then I wonder if I *would* have told her. While shopping and working out and swimming together, would we have talked about those things? The most important things in life? I hope so.

Now there's no chance it will happen. But there are other people around me—friends making choices similar to Diana's.

No, they aren't princesses or princes, but that's just what God wants to make them in His heavenly kingdom. I have to tell them.

"Delight yourself in the Lord and he will give you the desires of your heart. Commit your way to the Lord; trust in him and he will do this: he will make your righteousness shine like the dawn, the justice of your cause like the noonday sun" (Psalm 37:4-6).

Lori

Get off My Back

Last night I stood at the McDonald's counter in the mall, waiting for my strawberry shake. I might have been annoyed that five McDonald's employees were standing together behind the registers ignoring me, but I was too interested in the argument they were having with a woman customer.

"LOVE IS PATIENT."

The woman had waited 15 minutes for a burger, only to unwrap it and find it almost cold. She had then walked up and begun to complain, asking for her money back. The employees behind the counter, all about 14 or 15, had gotten upset with her attitude and were saying stuff like "We just made new burgers, so what's the problem?" and "I don't think McDonald's will close down just 'cause you're upset."

"LOVE IS KIND."

The woman came on pretty strong, and they weren't gonna take any Bolono from her. One kid started in at her with "Hey, are you upset? Are you upset? Come on, are you upset?" He was in her face big-time. He didn't use the old four-letter words out loud, but he meant them.

"IT IS NOT RUDE."

The manager wasn't any better at human relations; he just gave her the money and ignored what she was saying. He did say to the one kid who'd almost cussed her out, "You were doing it wrong," but he left it at that. Nobody learned anything.

"IT IS NOT SELF-SEEKING."

What about you? When someone's in your face for something you didn't do, do you stomp them? Every week of your life, perhaps every day, someone will accuse you, mistreat you, maybe misunderstand you. Human nature wants to fight back. Do you?

"IT IS NOT EASILY ANGERED."

You probably cannot stop yourself from becoming angry and rude when people get at you. A few control-freak type people can say to themselves, *I resolve to treat people fairly even when they are unfair or rude to me.* And they do it. But most people, like me, need God's help. I've learned from some fierce verbal wrestling matches that only God's spirit of love in my mind can control me.

"Love does not delight in evil but rejoices with the truth"
(1 Corinthians 13:6).

Tim

 Soul Care

My friend Dede sells skin-care products. "Hey, Lori," she said one day. "I need to schedule a party. Could you be a host? Do you know any people to invite?"

"Uh, sure, I know people," I answered.

"I mean, people besides the same people we all know—the same people we go to church with and work with."

"Oh."

"You know," she continued, "people in your neighborhood, people you're friends with outside our little circle of Adventists."

Suddenly she had given me a challenge. What friends do I have who aren't Seventh-day Adventists, just as I am?

Let's see. I go to a health club and work out four times a week. I see some of the same girls there, and we talk sometimes. But are we friends? Could I invite them to a party? hang out with them? I say hi to the people in my neighborhood when I walk by them, and I wave at them from inside my car. But have I even invited them into my house?

I had to tell Dede I couldn't host a party.

"You're like everyone else around here," she said. "We all have the same friends; we don't know anyone outside our circle. That's sad."

She's right. It's sad.

The next time the girls in step aerobics start talking about pigging out at Shoney's after a workout, I'm going to tell them to count me in. And maybe this year when the neighbors go through the subdivision Christmas caroling, I'll put on my coat, venture outside, and sing too.

I need more friends. Don't you?

"You are the light of the world. A city on a hill cannot be hidden. Neither do people light a lamp and put it under a bowl. Instead they put it on its stand, and it gives light to everyone in the house. In the same way, let your light shine before men, that they may see your good deeds and praise your Father in heaven" (Matthew 5:14-16).

Lori

Christmas in Heaven?

You may already know the sad story of Eric Clapton's son. After Clapton's rock-star life had shot through more twists than the Viper at Six Flags, he got clean and straight in the 1980s. In 1987 he had a son whom he named Conor.

One day in 1991 a maid left a window open in Clapton's fifty-third-floor apartment in New York City. Four-year-old Conor fell out of the window to his death. You've probably heard the song that came out of this tragedy, "Tears in Heaven."

For someone like Clapton, who has battled alcohol and heroin addiction, this must have been a severe blow and a great test. I have seen him play that song on TV, and I don't think I would have the strength to stand there and sing such a song.

I read recently that Clapton reportedly accepted Christ in 1969. He wrote a song called "Presence of the Lord" that at least one Christian artist has recorded. Since then Clapton has publicly denied and reaffirmed his faith several times. Only God knows where his heart is at now.

You might ask the question Why would God take away this boy? I think that's the wrong way to ask the question. We know from Jesus' example that God's way of life is to give and give and give. Sin and suffering and death are not God's way. These negative things are what take away our loved ones and our happiness.

I think the right way to ask the question is He's gone, so what next? If my Bible tells me correctly, the next big thing is heaven. The day we go to heaven will be a day of giving and receiving that we cannot begin to imagine.

I hope God gets the opportunity to give Eric Clapton his son back on that day, and I hope He gets the chance to give you all your loved ones. One gift He's already given is His Son, Jesus, and He's got infinitely more to give.

"Behold, I am coming soon! My reward is with me, and I will give to everyone according to what he has done" (Revelation 22:12).

Tim

Jesus Appears!

The picture caught my eye right away. Maybe because I recognized it. And I'm not used to recognizing pictures on magazines at the grocery-store checkout.

But here was that famous Harry Anderson painting of Jesus knocking on the United Nations building in New York. The same picture you've maybe seen on the paperback cover of *Steps to Christ.*

With the picture was this headline: 500-FOOT JESUS APPEARS AT UN.

And then it read: "Tourist takes snapshot of the image that will rock the world!" They even showed a picture of the tourist, Cloris McVeil, of Portland, Oregon.

As I opened the magazine to find the story, I caught some of the other headlines in the tabloid (these are for real—really):

"Boy, 10, Scares Mom to Death—Trying to Stop Her Hiccups."

"UFO Sucks the Eyeballs Out of 12 People!"

"Orange Juice Turns Violent Kids Into Little Angels."

"4-Legged Bride Marries Houston Plumber!" Says the bride, "He doesn't care about my extra legs. He just loves me for myself."

When I found the "story" behind the cover picture, I couldn't believe it. McVeil claims she took the picture and didn't notice anything unusual. But when she got her film developed, an image of Jesus appeared. "I almost fainted," she reports.

Sounds spooky, huh? But all the time I'm thinking, *This is a total joke!* Besides, it was an unauthorized and illegal use of an illustration to which the Review and Herald Publishing Association owns the copyright.

Somehow the story of Jesus' first arrival into this world as a baby in Bethlehem sounds more real. A lot more real. Maybe because so many people witnessed it and wrote about it. Maybe because it changed their lives. Maybe because there's something inside me that knows it's true.

And it's not spooky. It's kind of dramatic and humble and sweet. Kind of holy, you know?

My Bible's full of incredible stories like that one. But I bet you, like me, can tell there's something different between that book and tabloids like the *National Enquirer* and the *Weekly World News.*

There's something different about the story of Christ's picture appearing on someone's tourist photo—and Baby Jesus being born in a manger. And whose story you believe will make all the difference for you.

"The Word became flesh and made his dwelling among us. We have seen his glory, the glory of the One and Only, who came from the Father, full of grace and truth" (John 1:14).

Lori

How Will You Be Remembered?

Here's something to try. Draw a headstone on a piece of paper, and write out your epitaph. What do you want it to say about you?

Here lies _____, who died from _____ on _____. She/he lived a life of _____ and achieved _____. She/he is survived by _____.

You probably won't want your epitaph to say you died from complications of AIDS or an alcohol-related car wreck or lung cancer or a classmate's knife. You probably won't want it to record that you lived a life of addiction or apathy, or that you had no goals and achieved nothing. And you definitely don't want it to say you're survived by your whole family or your girlfriend or all of your friends or your hamster.

Yeah, I know. Many people die as victims of circumstances they can't control. But many die because they made choices that they felt were not right. You know the questions:

Should I study a lot or a little?

Should I smoke? Should I go to college or technical school?

Should I drive like the Road Runner on caffeine?

Should I go to church or hang out?

Should I volunteer?

Should I wait for sexual intimacy until I get married?
Should I drink this beer or skip it?
Should I always wear clothes that cover me up?
Should I believe in God and His promises?
Should I make quick cash selling pot?

Everything you do right now—even doing nothing—has consequences, sometimes life-and-death ones. The choices you make now will set up how your life will turn out.

So we shouldn't think only about the day of judgment at the end of the world. The consequences of most of our decisions come out into the open in this life even though we try to hide them. It may take a week or 20 years, but the effects show up all the same.

Plan now for the epitaph you *want,* not the one you might have to settle for.

"For God will bring every deed into judgment, including every hidden thing, whether it is good or evil" (Ecclesiastes 12:14).

Tim